MULTIMEDIA AND
GRAPHIC DESIGNERS

MULTIMEDIA AND GRAPHIC DESIGNERS
A Practical Career Guide

KEZIA ENDSLEY

ROWMAN & LITTLEFIELD
Lanham • Boulder • New York • London

Published by Rowman & Littlefield
An imprint of The Rowman & Littlefield Publishing Group, Inc.
4501 Forbes Boulevard, Suite 200, Lanham, Maryland 20706
www.rowman.com

6 Tinworth Street, London, SE11 5AL, United Kingdom

British Library Cataloguing in Publication Information Available

Library of Congress Cataloging-in-Publication Data

Names: Endsley, Kezia, 1968– author.
Title: Multimedia and graphic designers : a practical career guide / Kezia Endsley.
Description: Lanham : Rowman & Littlefield, [2020] | Series: Practical career guides |
    Includes bibliographical references and index. | Summary: "Multimedia & Graphic
    Designers: A Practical Career Guide includes interviews with professionals in a field that
    has proven to be a stable, lucrative, and growing profession"—Provided by publisher.
Identifiers: LCCN 2020003570 (print) | LCCN 2020003571 (ebook) | ISBN
    9781538133644 (paperback) | ISBN 9781538133651 (epub)
Subjects: LCSH: Commercial art—Vocational guidance. | Graphic arts—Vocational
    guidance. | Digital media—Vocational guidance.
Classification: LCC NC1001 .E53 2020 (print) | LCC NC1001 (ebook) | DDC
    740.023—dc23
LC record available at https://lccn.loc.gov/2020003570
LC ebook record available at https://lccn.loc.gov/2020003571

Contents

Introduction

Careers in Multimedia and Graphic Design

*W*elcome to a career in graphic design! If you are interested in a career as a graphic or multimedia artist, you've come to the right book. This book is an ideal place to start if you want to understand the various careers available to you in the field of multimedia and graphic design. It discusses what path you should follow to ensure you have all the training, education, and experience needed to succeed in your future career goals.

There is a lot of good news about this field. It's a great career choice for anyone with a desire to make a living using their creativity and artistic skills in a professional setting.

A career in multimedia and graphic design can be creative and fulfilling! ©valentinrussanov/E+/ Getty Images

When considering any career, your goal should be to find your specific nexus of interest, passion, and job demand. Although it is important to consider job outlook and demand, educational requirements, and other such practical matters, remember that you'll be spending a large portion of your life in whatever career you choose, so you should also find something that you enjoy doing and are passionate about. Especially when it comes to a creative profession like design, you need to have a passion for it. Of course, it can make the road easier to walk if you choose something that's in demand and pays the bills as well.

A Career in Graphic Design

Several professional titles and jobs fall under the umbrella of graphic design, including:

- Graphic designers
- Multimedia artists
- Web designers

Graphic design specialties can also be broken down based on the focus of the artist's work:

- Brand identity and logo design
- Packaging design
- Web and mobile design, including user experience and interface design
- Layout and print design

This book will discuss these main areas and the day-to-day responsibilities of each. Be sure to also check out the book *Computer Game Development & Animation*, by Tracy Brown Hamilton, for information related to careers in game design and animation.

So what exactly do graphic designers do on the job, day in and day out? What kind of skills and educational background do you need to succeed in this field? How much can you expect to make, and what are the pros and cons of each area? How do you determine if graphic design is a good fit for you, and which kind of design best fits your talents and interests? This book can help you answer these questions and more.

For each of these areas of graphic design, the book covers the pros and cons, the educational requirements, projected annual wages, personality traits that are well suited, working conditions and expectations, and more. You'll even read some interviews from real designers working in these industries. The goal is for you to learn enough about multimedia and graphic design to give you a clear view as to which career path, if any, is a good fit for you. And if you still have more questions, this book will also point you to resources where you can learn even more.

"I went into this career because I love it and wanted to do it. It's not something to do if you're purely money driven. Some people can make good money, but the majority won't get rich. Go into it because you have a love for the art and want a creative career."—Kim Kultgen, graphic designer

The Market Today

The US Bureau of Labor Statistics (BLS) is part of the US Department of Labor. It tracks statistical information about thousands of careers in the United States. The BLS forecasts that the graphic design market will grow at about 3 percent between 2018 and 2028, which is less than the average job growth rate.[1] The market for multimedia artists is projected to grow about 4 percent[2] and the market for website designers is projected to grow about 13 percent.[3]

There are many factors that affect the US demand for jobs in design, some favorable and others not. Consider these current issues:

- The use of print materials continues to shrink as more and more information is presented visually on phones and computer screens; as a result the print publishing industry is declining. In fact, employment of graphic designers in newspaper, periodical, book, and directory publishers is projected to decline 22 percent between 2018 and 2028.[4]
- Employment of graphic designers in computer systems design and related services is projected to grow 24 percent over that same period![5]

- Companies are continuing to increase their digital presence, requiring graphic designers to help create visually appealing and effective websites.

The bottom line is that your job prospects will be best if you keep up with the latest design trends, technologies, and techniques. Chapter 1 covers lots more about the job prospects in these areas and breaks down the numbers for each area into more detail.

What Does This Book Cover?

The goal of this book is to cover all aspects of graphic and multimedia design and explain the differences between the various areas and how you can excel in them. Here's a breakdown of the chapters:

- Chapter 1 explains the different careers under the umbrella of graphic design that are covered in this book. You'll learn about what graphic designers and multimedia artists do in their day-to-day work, the different environments in which graphic designers work, some pros and cons about each, the average salaries of these jobs, and the general outlook for design in the future.
- Chapter 2 explains in detail the educational requirements of these different areas, from bachelor's degrees to master's degrees and beyond. You will learn how to go about getting experience (in the form of internships, for example) in these various settings before you enter college as well as during your college years.
- Chapter 3 explains all the aspects of college and postsecondary schooling that you'll want to consider as you move forward. You will learn about the great schools out there and how to get the best education for the best deal. You will also learn a little about scholarships and financial aid and how the SAT and ACT work.
- Chapter 4 covers all aspects of the résumé-writing and interviewing processes, including creating a dynamic portfolio that conveys your unique creative style, writing a stellar résumé and cover letter, interviewing to your best potential, dressing for the part, communicating effectively, and more.

Where Do You Start?

You can approach the graphic design field in a few different ways—you can come to the field from a creative artist perspective and focus on a fine arts degree, or you can focus on computer programming and development and come to the career from a more technical angle. In either case, you will need to meld the creative and artistic with knowledge of technologies as they change in our evolving digital world.

Your future awaits! ©Delpixart/iStock/Getty Images Plus

The good news is that you don't need to know the answers to these questions yet. In order to find the best fit for yourself in graphic design, you need to understand how these different career areas are structured. That's where you'll start in chapter 1.

Why Choose a Career in Multimedia and Graphic Design?

You learned in the introduction that the graphic design field continues to focus more and more on digital online approaches. You learned that your best prospects for success mean you need to learn and keep up with technology. You also were reminded that it's important to pursue a career that you enjoy, are good at, and are passionate about. You will spend a lot of your life working; it makes sense to find something you enjoy doing. Of course, you want to make money and support yourself while doing it. If you love the idea of being creative for a living, you've come to the right book.

This chapter breaks out the job areas that typically fall under the graphic design umbrella and covers the basics of each. After reading this chapter, you should have a good understanding of the various areas of multimedia design and can then start to determine if one of them is a good fit for you. Let's start with discussing what a graphic designer actually does on the job.

What Do Graphic Designers Do?

When you think of a multimedia or graphic designer, you may picture a person working on a laptop, creating brochures and marketing materials in a program like InDesign; someone working in a program like Photoshop to create icons and other graphics for use or display; or someone writing HTML, CCS, and other code to create attractive websites. Graphic designers can do all these things and more.

In addition to the different programs and technologies they use, the work of multimedias artist and graphic designers varies greatly depending on the field they work in, the purpose of their projects (to sell something, to evoke

No matter what type of graphic design you do, you will certainly design your models on-screen.
©NicoElNino/iStock/Getty Images Plus

emotion, to convince, etc.), the media in which they work, and more. That's good news, because it means there are a lot of choices and variation in these fields. To maximize your career options, you need to make sure you have the right degree and continue to educate yourself about changes in the field. Chapters 2 and 3 cover the educational requirements in more depth.

WHAT QUALITIES DO YOU NEED TO SUCCEED IN GRAPHIC DESIGN?

Regardless of whether you're leaning more toward graphic design, multimedia design, web design, user interface design, or some mix of all of these, there is a core list of important qualities you'll need to have, or at least sharpen over time:

- *Artistic talent:* You need artistic ability and a good understanding of color, texture, and light; however, you may be able to compensate for artistic shortcomings with excellent technical skills.

- *Communication skills:* You need to work as part of a team, be able to convey your ideas articulately, and compromise when needed.
- *Analytical skills:* You must be able to perceive your work from a consumer or client point of view to ensure that the designs convey the intended message.
- *Computer skills:* You will very likely use computer programs or write programming code to do most of your work.
- *Creativity:* You must be able to think creatively to develop original ideas and help them come to life.
- *Concentration:* You must sit at a computer and write detailed code for long periods.
- *Thick skin:* You must be able to respond well to criticism and feedback and learn not to take it personally, even when it's your personal vision that's being rejected.
- *Time-management skills:* Workdays can be long, particularly when there are tight deadlines; you'll need to be able to manage your time effectively when a deadline is approaching.

Most of these skills can be refined and polished with experience, education, and hard work, so don't worry if you feel like you're not quite there yet. If a career in graphic design is what you want, perseverance is key!

TRADITIONAL GRAPHIC DESIGNERS

In the most general sense, graphic designers use 2D or 3D art to create visual concepts that inspire, inform, and captivate users. They work on logos and layout designs for magazines, brochures, reports, advertisements, and more. They create designs, but they also have to consider things like negative space, readability, and typography.

Sometimes also called layout artists, they design the structure of text and images in good-looking format, often for printed forms of media. Other typical positions or titles that graphic designers hold include creative director, art director, art production manager, brand identity developer, and illustrator.

They overwhelmingly work in studios, where they have access to equipment such as drafting tables, computers, and software. Although many graphic designers work independently as freelancers, those who work for specialized graphic design firms are often part of a creative team. Many graphic designers collaborate with colleagues or work with clients on projects.

According to the Bureau of Labor Statistics, in 2018 about 20 percent of graphic designers worked for themselves as freelancers; 10 percent worked in specialized design services (such as architectural, engineering, scientific, and other technical fields); 8 percent worked in advertising, public relations, and related services; 7 percent worked in print support; and 5 percent worked for newspaper, periodical, book, and directory publishers.

Traditional graphic designers create projects for their employer or for clients. Some of their responsibilities include:

- Planning a visual concept by studying materials and understanding the big-picture approach
- Illustrating a concept by creating a rough layout of art and copy; this usually includes the arrangement, size, and style of all elements
- Creating guidelines for how logos and other branding materials should be displayed and used
- Helping to make design choices (e.g., fonts and colors) for all content the company will use
- Preparing final copy and art by operating typesetting, printing, and similar equipment
- Completing projects on time by coordinating with outside agencies, art services, printers, and so on
- Maintaining technical knowledge by attending design workshops, reviewing professional publications, and participating in professional societies
- Working with other creative team members to produce content and get results, as needed

In addition to working well with others on a team, graphic designers need to be creative, flexible, deadline oriented, and detail oriented, and be able to take criticism and handle feedback.

"Learn to take criticism. You must have a solid ego so you can take criticism and learn from it."—Jill Flores, graphic designer

MULTIMEDIA ARTISTS AND ANIMATORS

This book differentiates between more traditional graphic designers and multimedia artists. Multimedia artists and animators create images and models that appear to move, as well as visual effects for television, movies, video games, and other forms of media. They usually specialize in one arena or medium; for example, some create animated movies or video games, whereas others create visual effects for companies or for entertainment purposes. They might create computer-generated images (CGI) or design scenery or backgrounds.

Multimedia artists and animators typically create their work using computer software or by writing computer code. Many animation companies even have their own computer animation software that their artists must learn to use. It's very important for you to learn and hone your skills in computer graphics in order to compete in this field.

Video game artists also fit into this genre. They focus on creating the look, feel, and layout of a video game. Video game designers work in a variety of platforms, including mobile gaming and online social networks. Check out the book *Computer Game Development and Animation* for more information about that profession.

Multimedia artists and animators typically:

- Use computer programs to create graphics and animation
- Work with a team of animators and artists to create a game or visual effect
- Research upcoming projects to help create realistic designs or animation
- Edit animation and effects based on feedback

If you work in this industry, you will very likely be expected to work well in a team settng, where you will develop graphics, animations, or visual effects in cooperation with others who work on other aspects of the project. Each animator essentially works on a portion of the project, and then the pieces are put together to create a cohesive final product.

WHAT QUALITIES DO YOU NEED TO BE AN ARTIST?

Just like other careers, if you bring certain personal qualities to the profession of graphic artist, you will greatly increase your chances of both artistic success and career success.

- *Creativity:* Creativity is the ability to make something new. Creativity is problem solving. It means looking at things differently, considering many options, trying and discarding ideas, and then making something new.

    Talent and creativity are related but a little different. Talent is what comes naturally to you, while creativity can cross over into anything that you do.

- *Drive:* Drive is that inner feeling that pushes you to do the thing you care about most. Drive can be strong or quiet, fast or slow, subtle or overpowering.

    Drive gives you the confidence to believe in your ideas enough to voice them. Drive makes you want to do better, to "fail up," to learn from your mistakes, to improve your skills, to delve more deeply into your ideas.

- *Persistence:* Persistence means you keep going. You'll need persistence at every level, from learning art skills to finishing artwork to building a portfolio to getting your work in front of people. Persistence means pushing forward when outside influences are pushing back.

    The good news is that persistence is a skill that you can teach yourself. So how do you become persistent?

- Know your goals. It's easier to keep moving if you can see where you're going.
- Keep your goals reachable. How do you eat an elephant? One bite at a time. Don't frighten yourself with large, distant goals. Instead, focus on the next thing you need to do: turn an assignment in on time, critique a website, create a logo, and so on.
- Know your priorities. You already know what your priorities are. Get your schoolwork done. Get your work-work done. Hang with your friends. Call your mom. And create designs. (Not necessarily in that order.)
- Make design a priority. Take time to study design all around you, and be sure to carve out time in your schedule to work on your own designs.
- Use positive self-talk. Don't let your inner voice give you a hard time. We all have a nasty little inner voice that makes us doubt ourselves. Counter

that voice by purposely talking to yourself in a supportive and positive way. No, not out loud. Tell yourself, "I'm just going to do this now."

- Get in the habit of getting in the habit. Pick a thing and do it. Then pick another thing and do that. Repeat.
- Notice when you finish. Pay attention to those special times when you complete a project. Feel proud of yourself. See how nice that is? Noticing how good it feels to finish something helps you be persistent in the future.
- *Patience:* Creating something from nothing takes patience at every stage. Patience doesn't mean sitting around waiting for opportunities to come to you. Patience means accepting that things take time and that fretting and stressing about things doesn't make them happen any sooner. Patience means accepting that if one opportunity doesn't work out, there is always another one.
- *Faith in yourself and your work:* Perhaps the most important quality designers need is to have faith in themselves as artists and faith in their work. Some people seem to be born confident or talented or both. Others need to develop it over the course of a lifetime.

  Faith in yourself doesn't mean arrogance, or the assumption that you have nothing new or different to learn. It means an internal confidence in your ability to learn, to imagine, and to create that will carry you during difficult times. It means learning to recognize what is good in your work yourself, without relying only on the opinions of others. It also means being confident enough in your abilities to recognize when a design is not working so that you can either fix it or set it aside and move on to something else.

WEB DESIGNERS AND DEVELOPERS

Web designers and developers get their own category because of the specialized skills and knowledge needed in this area as well as the different job demands, pay, and job outlook than the more traditional graphic artist.

This profession is varied and broad, and can be largely broken into three main areas, depending on which aspect of the website artists are responsible for:

- *Front-end web developers:* These designers are essentially responsible for how a website looks. They focus on the site's layout, which could include graphics, applications, interactive icons, and more. They are responsible for implementing the agreed-upon design on the website using languages like Hypertext Markup Language (HTML), cascading stylesheets (CSS), and JavaScript.

- *Backend web developers:* These designers focus on the server-side development, which are the behind-the-scenes activities that happen when a user performs an action on a website: for example, logging in to an account or purchasing a watch from an online store. They focus on databases, scripting, and the architecture of websites. They write code to communicate the database information to the browser.[1]
- *Webmasters:* These folks ensure that the website works as it should and test for errors such as broken links. Many webmasters respond to user comments and monitor and report on traffic through the site.

Keep in mind that these aren't always separate jobs. In a small company or start-up, the web designer/developer may be responsible for all of these tasks. That means you'll need some technical know-how, often including a bachelor's degree in computer science, programming, or a related field and a thorough understanding of HTML and other web programming languages. Chapter 2 covers the educational expectations in more detail.

Focusing on a Design Specialty

The multimedia and graphic design field can also be approached from the focus of the design and creative efforts, as mentioned in the introduction. For the purposes of this book, we have broken these into four main areas—brand identity and logo design, packaging design, web and mobile design, and layout and print design. Let's look at each of these in more detail.

BRAND IDENTITY AND LOGO DESIGN

Graphic designers in this arena are responsible for envisioning, recommending, and designing original and effective visual identities for new and existing brands, organizations, products, and services. Along with fonts and colors, logos are key to brand identity. This type of graphic design requires the design team to be able to create a unique selection and arrangement of colors, shapes, and designs that will be used to represent a brand nearly everywhere, from websites to company buildings to advertisements.

These designers may also need to produce business cards, letterhead, ads, and many other different types of graphic design outputs featuring the new brand identity.[2]

PACKAGING DESIGN

Designers who work in packaging design must be able to design 3D shapes, including the inside and outside of the product packaging. This designer's job is to create designs that protect the product in shipping, catch the eye of potential consumers, and then, when viewed up close, inform and persuade them to buy the product.

This type of design involves not only creating initial sketches and computer work, but also testing your design on physical mock-ups. An understanding of packaging materials and their environmental impact is also important in package design.[3]

WEB AND MOBILE DESIGN

This area was discussed in depth earlier in the chapter. Artists in web and mobile design can focus on either of these two different areas, as long as they know the standards and best practices of the medium for which they're designing. Knowing the basics of coding is important in this career. More specialized roles in web and mobile design include user experience design and user interface design.[4]

LAYOUT AND PRINT DESIGN

Artists who focus on layout and print design use software like InDesign, Photoshop, Illustrator, and Acrobat. The goal is to find the perfect balance between text and graphics by creating designs that are both aesthetically pleasing and easy to read. Print media includes magazines, books, newspapers, brochures, posters, and more.

The placement of images and the selection of font and typeface is of particular concern to layout and print designers, especially when working with large amounts of text. Familiarity with printing processes and production is also essential for success in this career.[5]

The Pros and Cons of the Multimedia and Graphic Design Field

As with any career, one in graphic design has upsides and downsides. But also true is that one person's pro is another person's con. If you love working in teams and collaborating with others, then this could well be the right job for you; if you prefer to work solo, it's probably going to be frustrating for you at times. If you like the rush of a hurried deadline, ever-changing specifications, and due dates, and don't mind working long hours at times, then you will get a charge out of graphic design.

Although it's one thing to read about the pros and cons of a particular career, the best way to really get a feel for what a typical day is like on the job and what the challenges and rewards are is to talk to someone who is working in the profession. You can also learn a lot by reading the interviews with actual designers that you find throughout this book.

Although each profession within multimedia and graphic design is different, some generalizations can be made when it comes to what is most challenging and most gratifying about the field.

"Keeping on top of all the digital trends and making sure your creativity works for social media is important and can be challenging. You have to keep on top of it and keep abreast of the latest technology."—Sue Porritt, graphic designer

Some general pros include:

- You get to do what you love: animating, designing, creating art, laying out your vision, and so on. You get to apply your technical, artistic, or business skills to an industry you have a real passion for.
- The work tends to be creative and challenging.
- In this competitive field, you will have colleagues who share your passion and from whom you can learn.
- It is a constantly evolving field with new trends and innovations and an endless opportunity for learning.
- There's a vast degree of variety in work environments, from large corporations to start-ups to freelance work from anywhere.
- It's a field you can enter without necessarily having a college degree, although it's easier to get your foot in the door if you have one.

Some general cons include:

- The working hours can be long and irregular. You can expect at times to work early and late hours and also on weekends in order to meet pressing deadlines or deal with any number of unpredictable issues or situations that may arise.
- Because of the high degree of collaboration, artists, writers, or developers—anyone on the team—can expect to have to surrender an idea or even a whole design that they feel attached to. You have to be flexible and think as a team member rather than as an individual creator.
- It is high-pressure field that requires an ability to manage stress well and to multitask. You need a thick skin in order to be able to handle criticism and feedback.
- It is an extremely competitive field. Breaking in and advancing to the next level can take a lot of time, hard work, creativity, and patience.
- Some areas of graphic design (such as print) are experiencing negative growth as publishing and print materials in general are becoming less desirable.

The good news is that you can control some of the above factors. You can eliminate or mitigate many of these drawbacks by carefully choosing the environment you work in. For example, to ensure you have good job prospects and

Collaborating with other smart and creative people who you respect can be one of the great joys of graphic design. ©adimguzhva/iStock/Getty Images Plus

enter a healthy field, you can focus on web or mobile design rather than print design.

How Healthy Is the Job Market?

Recall from the introduction that the Bureau of Labor Statistics, which is part of the US Department of Labor, tracks statistical information about thousands of careers in the United States. Data about careers in graphic design differ greatly depending on the area of focus/approach. Let's look at each one separately.

WEB AND MOBILE DEVELOPERS AND DESIGNERS

- *Education:* Varies from an associate's degree in web design or related field to a bachelor's degree in computer science or programming
- *2018 median pay:* $69,430
- *Job outlook 2018–2028:* 13 percent (much faster than average)

- *Work environment:* In the computer systems design and related services industry; some are self-employed and others work in industries including publishing, management consulting, and advertising[6]

MULTIMEDIA ARTISTS AND ANIMATORS

- *Education:* Bachelor's degree in computer graphics, art, or a related field and a strong portfolio
- *2018 median pay:* $72,520
- *Job outlook 2018–2028:* 4 percent (as fast as average)
- *Work environment:* Work in offices for companies or self-employed[7]

GRAPHIC DESIGNERS

- *Education:* Bachelor's degree in graphic design, art, or a related field and a strong portfolio
- *2018 median pay:* $50,370
- *Job outlook 2018–2028:* 3 percent (slower than average)
- *Work environment:* Many are employed in specialized design services, publishing, or advertising, public relations, and related services industries[8]

Note that this general category includes brand identity and logo design, package design, and print design, the last of which is declining at a higher rate than any other area of graphic design. In fact, employment of graphic designers in newspaper, periodical, book, and directory publishers is projected to decline 22 percent between 2018 and 2028; however, employment of graphic designers in computer systems design and related services is projected to grow 24 percent over the same period.[9] You can be sure that you are on the right side of that trend by immersing yourself in computer systems design.

Are you interested in video game design? It is admittedly a highly competitive field, but if you have the creative vision and the technical know-how, it can be a lucrative and enjoyable one too. The annual wage in 2018 was $72,000[10] and the projected growth of this career is 12 percent, which is faster than average.[11]

If you remember anything from this chapter, the biggest takeaway is that the market is viable and healthy when you approach it from a technical, computer graphics perspective.

DANIELLE FOSTER: PRINT LAYOUT DESIGNER

Danielle Foster. *Courtesy of Danielle Foster*

Danielle Foster graduated with a bachelor's degree in art, with an emphasis in graphic design, from San Diego State University. Computers weren't being used in graphic design at that time; everything was done by hand. Danielle then went to Platt College to learn to use computers. She worked for a magazine about digital art, and that publisher was asked to do a book about multimedia. That led to other work in book publishing. Her husband got a job at that publisher (Prima Publishing) and she free-lanced there as well. She had only worked in the field for maybe two years before she began freelancing. She had a child soon after, so she kept freelancing through the good times and the bad. All her work has been in book publishing.

Can you explain how you became interested in graphic design?

When I was in high school, I was on the yearbook staff, which I really enjoyed. I took a career aptitude test, and I tested high for graphic design. But I didn't really know what that was. I went to college for business, but didn't like it. I then started taking art classes and really enjoyed them. I have a creative and a mathematical brain, and I think it's a combo of those. I am not as artistic as some, but I am organized and on task. I can focus better than some more creative types.

Can you talk about your current position?

I am still a full-time freelancer in book design. Freelancing is not for everyone, but I love it. Most book publishers have templates, so the true creative design work was already done. They give their design to me, their Word files, and the images, which have [already] been created. I get the pieces and put the puzzle together. I make sure it looks the way it is supposed to, is in the right place, fits the guidelines, and is ready for the printing process. Timeliness is very important. Deadlines are always looming, and I am the last person in the process so often I am making up for lost time. Getting the book laid out on time is very important. I mostly use InDesign, Acrobat, Photoshop, and Illustrator. Being detail oriented is very important too.

What's the best part of being a graphic designer?

I really like that it's different every time, but always the same skill set. My job doesn't feel super repetitive. I like working from home, especially when my son was little. I could have been happy doing a lot of different things. But I do enjoy it, and the time goes by fast. It just fits me. I feel like it's creative enough for me. I am not super artistic, but I like the details and I like the control.

What is the hardest part of your job and why?

The hardest part is the uncertainty of work, because I freelance. Not having health-care and other benefits as well.

Meeting deadlines and relying on other people to get you what you need is also challenging. Always having to look for new work can be difficult. Art is subjective, so someone might not like what you do. You have to be willing to do what clients want even if you don't really like it. You have to put your ego to the side.

What are some things in this profession that are especially challenging right now?

Work is sometimes sent overseas because they can do it cheaper. It's ever-changing, and you always have to keep up with technology. If you are on the creative end, you can get stuck sometimes and can't think of good ideas. Also, the stress of deadlines in larger firms can be challenging—or rewarding if you like that pressure.

What are some characteristics of a good graphic designer?

I think that depends on what kind of graphic design you pursue, but creativity is toward the top of the list. Being a creative problem solver. Having artistic talent, at least an eye for what is good and what doesn't work. There also needs to be a part of you that's "techie" and enjoys the technical side of things, especially now. Like production—you lay it out. It's not your idea, but you create it. Then you work your way into coming up with the ideas.

I feel like I am more like a craftsperson than an artist.

What advice do you have for young people considering this career?

This career can be so many different things. Make sure you have a decent idea of what it is and have some acumen for it. You can take it anywhere, which is nice.

To see if you like it, try using Adobe software at school. Do yearbook or newspaper at school. Dip your toe and see if you like it. Look all around you—anything you see that's printed or online is graphic design. Even the grocery store is full of graphic design! Be aware that it's not always just about being creative. It takes creativity, but that's not all it takes.

How can a young person prepare for a career in graphic design while in high school?

Talk to the art teachers at your high school and get their perspective on it. See graphic design in action in your town. Reach out to designers or look on Craigslist to see who is advertising for designers in your area. Contact them and ask if you can come in and job shadow. Shadowing will show you a day in the life and help you see past the glamour. You don't have to go to college. You can teach yourself and find books to teach yourself. Trade schools teach it too. If you're artistic, you can build your portfolio on your own. Take online classes and build your portfolio that way. You'll make and build projects. That's cheaper and doesn't require academic hoops to jump through. You can do that while working a 9-to-5 job, even, if you're motivated. Student editions of the Adobe suite are available! Don't be intimidated by having to go to college. College is not for everyone.

The main thing is, if you're a kid who is creative but also can stay on task, this is a good career for you. You have to be able to handle a project and get it done by the deadline.

―――――――

Would I Be a Good Graphic Designer?

This is a tough question to answer, because really the answer can only come from you. But don't despair: There are plenty of resources both online and elsewhere that can help you find the answer by guiding you through the types of questions and considerations that will bring you to your conclusion.

Of course no job is going to match your personality or fit your every desire, especially when you are just starting out. There are, however, some aspects to a job that may be so unappealing or simply mismatched that you may decide to opt for something else, or you may be so drawn to a feature of a job that any downsides are not that important.

Obviously having an ability and a passion for art, design, or programming in any capacity is key to success in this field, but there are other factors to keep in mind. One way to see if you may be cut out for this career is to ask yourself the following questions:

- *Am I a highly creative person who is also able to let an idea I may love go because others disagree or it just isn't possible?*
  Any creative person feels attached to his or her ideas. When you are working alone on your own vision—be it a book, a painting, a game, or what have you—you have full control over what the end result will be. It doesn't work that way when you work creatively with a team and when you have a client who has a different vision and the ultimate say in how things look.
- *Am I able to follow directions even if I don't agree? Am I able to understand instructions quickly?*
  Working in a team can be a fulfilling and inspiring experience, and this field does provide that for the most part. However, it does require being comfortable with others making final decisions and understanding quickly what you are tasked with doing.
- *Can I create good designs under tight deadlines?*
  Working under tight deadlines can be exhilarating, but it can also cause you to experience moments of "idea freeze." Can you work through those creative morasses? Are you willing to work some long hours and weekends when needed?
- *When something goes wrong, can I think quickly on my feet to find a solution? Do I have the leadership skills to direct others to problem solve?*
  Because this is a fast-paced industry where everything can change at any time, being flexible and staying calm under pressure is paramount. Equally important is being able to provide solutions or suggestions when something goes awry.
- *Can I consistently deal with people in a professional, friendly way?*
  Communication is a key skill to have in any profession, but particularly as a designer, because it's important to convey clearly and concisely what your expectations and visions are.

If the answer to any of these questions is an adamant *no*, you might want to consider a different path. Remember that learning what you *don't* like can be just as important as figuring out what you *do* like to do.

Are you ready for a creative and rewarding career in graphic design? ©mediaphotos/iStock/Getty Images Plus

If you pursue a career that fundamentally conflicts with the person you are, you won't be good at it and you won't be happy. Don't make that mistake. If you need help in determining your key personality factors, you can take a career counseling questionnaire to find out more. You can find many online or ask you school guidance counselor for reputable sources.

CHRIS SHUTE: CREATIVE DIRECTOR AND BRANDING EXPERT

Chris Shute started his creative education at Herron Art School during his senior year of high school. During that time, he built his portfolio to get into postsecondary art school. He went to a traditional college for two years, then moved to the Art

Chris Shute. *Courtesy of Chris Shute*

Academy of Cincinnati and earned a BFA in marketing and adverting.

His first job was in Nashville, Tennessee, in country music entertainment promotions (from T-shirt design to albums to concert poster design); it included NASCAR marketing and advertising design. He spent two years there.

He then moved back to Indiana and became a marketing director for a direct-mail marketing firm, where he spent four years before deciding he wanted to work for a traditional ad agency.

He worked for small- to medium-sized ad firms. This included campaign writing, advertising, and headline writing. It was the media of the day—outdoor, print ads, TV commercials, and radio. He got bigger and bigger clients, including medical device branding and design as well as national brands and companies.

He started at his current job in 1998. He works at a small firm, so he can directly interface with clients and create and nurture relationships directly. He likes having more control over the clients and their expectations.

Can you explain how you became interested in graphic design?

I loved drawing and art as a kid. I don't think of myself as a true fine artist, but I loved telling stories using pictures. I loved getting pads of paper for gifts and just kept drawing. I also loved coming up with stories. Fiction, horror, and comedy, it didn't matter—I loved telling stories with pictures. Even in grade school, I did ads. I saw TV ads and thought I could do better.

Advertising was just something I gravitated to. I had a talent for it. I could draw and could put ideas on paper that others would respond to. I had good rapport with art teachers and I won some contests here and there. It all kept growing my confidence in my ability. In fact, I still draw and enjoy working in pencil. I love Western art and like drawing images that evoke strong emotion.

Can you talk about your current position? What is your title? What do you do day to day?

Creative director is my title. A small agency doesn't really have titles, but that would be it. It's all encompassing and big picture. The understanding and knowing what to ask, when to listen, when to be quiet, and when to advise. Understanding the product/service or objective and then setting the tone with messaging or imaging. Then I direct all the players needed to actually execute the process—videographers, photographers, writers, web developers, artists, printers, TV stations, and so on. I am the owner of it and make sure it's all in line and consistent with what the client wants. I also pitch the idea at the beginning.

The art director brings the creative director's big ideas and vision to life. The creative director is more concerned about the big picture.

I enjoy helping companies brand and rebrand themselves. I like to help a small company that's had a lot of success figure out how to fine-tune their brand after they have outgrown their original concept. This encompasses design, collateral, website content, and beyond. You build a good story. Storytelling is important with branding. Taking a company that's outgrown their brand and bringing them forward to the new concept is challenging but also really enjoyable.

What's the best part of being a graphic designer?

Being able to do what I like and am good at and make a living. This is my natural talent. This is all I enjoyed. A true affinity and ability for the job can lead to good rewards—more money, your ideas are fun to see come to life, and collaboration with other people is rewarding.

It takes collaboration and communication to make a good idea a great one. If everyone wants to make it better, the idea will grow and get better. If it's only personal opinion, it's a difficult process. You have to be open-minded and know that a great idea can come from anywhere but is made better by a team. I enjoy that collaboration.

What is the hardest part of your job and why?

Working with a client who doesn't understand what we do and might not value what we do is challenging. They have unrealistic expectations, so you might spend a lot of your time convincing them about what they need. If they aren't open to real change, it's an uphill battle. They think they want it, but then pull back and don't let marketing reach the potential that you know it could.

When you are starting off, there's a lot of uncertainty—where do you start, where are there jobs, how can you get your foot in the door, will your ideas get accepted, are you good enough, are you as good as your peers. It's pretty competitive and can be cutthroat. People's egos get in the way.

What are some things in this profession that are especially challenging right now?

Longevity is difficult in this business. You need real perseverance to break in and succeed. You can lose your enthusiasm. You have to stay in it to succeed.

Finding clients that value what you do and are willing to pay for it to do it well. Budgets are always a problem. Finding the right budgets for the projects and cost expectations. Marketing is often the first thing that companies cut when things are bad. Companies have found ways to do more with less since the recession—especially with small to midsize companies.

What are some characteristics of a good graphic designer?

Having a thick skin is important. Being a good listener and understanding that the client isn't "wrong." You have to see the other side of the coin. Clients know all about their products, of course, but they often don't know why people want them. A good design will find their audience and the benefit, and then create a story so the audience says, "Aha, I need that." A good designer will design to that. It's all about the buyer/client and who they are selling to. If they have that in their mind, it works.

What advice do you have for young people considering this career?

Have perseverance, stay tough, and hang in there. It's not a sprint—you are in it for the long haul. If you hone your skills and continue to grow and understand what it takes to succeed, you'll do well. You have to continually do it—live it, breathe it, etc. You have to be dedicated to it.

Strive for better work and don't get your feelings in it. Learn to take criticism. Be tough. Some of it's very valuable and you need to be open minded to hear it. Critique in art is a hard thing—you have to build up your skin.

How can a young person prepare for a career in graphic design while in high school?

Take all the art classes that you can. Also, creative writing, radio station, and TV production classes if you can. Understanding psychology is also important for marketing skills. Try to get into a company to shadow or intern, even just to make copies. Get in so you hear the lingo and see how the profession really works. If you have code development, you can help update code, use WordPress, and so on.

Any last thoughts?

Web development, social media, app development, and digital tools in general are all key components of web design. I look at them as tools in the toolbox. Digital media is one of the biggest tools today. Understanding how online ads work, learning how a website's user interface works, and being able to create apps that make it fun to engage with a product are all key components.

A website is a tool; social media is a tool. You must understand them in a broad sense to know what they provide to your client.

It's not an easy field. It's competitive and tight. You have to stick with it, hone your skills, and sell yourself and your ideas. Learn how to stand up in front of people. Learn how to be comfortable in front of a crowd and speak with conviction. If you waffle, your clients will sense that, and they will waffle too. But it has to be real.

—————

Summary

In this chapter, you learned a lot about the different types of careers that exist under the general graphic design umbrella. You've learned about what multimedia artists do in comparison with web and mobile designers and print designers, for example. You also learned about some pros and cons of this field, the average salaries of these jobs, and the outlook in the future for various areas of graphic design. You hopefully even contemplated some questions about whether your personal likes and preferences meld well with this career. Are you starting to get excited about the idea of being a graphic designer? If not, that's okay, as there's still time.

Chapter 2 dives into forming a plan for your future, covering everything there is to know about educational requirements, certifications, internship opportunities, and more, about each of these areas of graphic design. You'll learn about finding summer jobs and how to start building an amazing portfolio that has your own unique sensibility as well. The goal is for you to set yourself apart—and above—the rest.

2

Forming a Career Plan

*I*t's not easy to choose a career, yet it's one of the most important decisions you will make in your life. There are simply so many options available, and it is easy to feel overwhelmed. Particularly if you have many passions and interests, it can be hard to narrow your options down. That you are reading this book means you have decided to investigate a career in the graphic design industry, which means you have already discovered a passion for creativity, technology, and ongoing learning. But even within the graphic design industry, there are many choices, including what role you want to pursue, what work environment you desire, and what type of work schedule best fits your lifestyle.

Now that you have some idea about the different career opportunities within the graphic design umbrella, it's time to formulate a career plan. For you organized folks out there, this can be a helpful and energizing process. If you're not a naturally organized person, or if the idea of looking ahead and building a plan to adulthood scares you, you are not alone. That's what this chapter is for.

After discussing ways to develop a career plan—there is more than one way to do this!—the chapter dives into the various educational requirements. Finally, it looks at how you can gain experience through school activities such as the high school yearbook and newspaper, job shadowing, volunteering, part-time jobs, and more. Yes, experience will look good on your résumé, and in some cases it's even required, but even more important, getting out there and working in graphic design in various settings is the best way to determine if it's really something that you will enjoy. When you find a career that you truly enjoy and have a passion for, it will rarely feel like work at all.

If you still aren't sure if the graphic design field is right for you, try a self-assessment questionnaire or a career aptitude test. There are many good ones on the web. As an example, the career resource website Monster.com includes free self-assessment tools at www.monster.com/career-advice/article/best-free-career-assessment-tools. The Princeton Review also has a very good aptitude test geared toward high schoolers at www.princetonreview.com/quiz/career-quiz.

Your ultimate goal should be to match your personal interests and goals with your preparation plan for college and career. Practice articulating your plans and goals to others. When you feel comfortable speaking about your aspirations, that means you have a good grasp of your goals and your plan to reach them.

Planning the Plan

The following points are helpful to think about deeply when planning your career path.

- Think about your interests outside of the work context. How do you like to spend your free time? What inspires you? What kind of people do you like to surround yourself with, and how do you best learn? What do you really love doing?
- Brainstorm a list of the various career choices within the graphic design industry that you are interested in pursuing. Organize the list in order of which careers you find most appealing, and then list what it is about each that attracts you. This can be anything from work environment to geographical location to the degree to which you would work with other people in a particular role.
- Research each job on your career choices list. You can find job descriptions, salary indications, career outlook, salary, and educational requirements information online.
- Consider your personality traits. How do you respond to stress and pressure? Do you consider yourself a strong communicator? Do you work well in teams or prefer to work independently? Do you consider yourself creative? How do you respond to criticism? It is important to keep these in mind to ensure you choose a career path that makes you happy and in which you can thrive.
- Although your choice of career is obviously a huge factor in your future, it's important to consider what other factors feature in your vision of your ideal life. Think about how your career will fit in with the rest of your life, including whether you want to live in a big city or small town, how much flexibility you want in your schedule, how much autonomy you want in your work, and what your ultimate career goal is.

- Graphic design is a very competitive field, particularly when you are starting out in your career. Because it requires so much commitment, it's important to think about how willing you are to put in long hours and perform what can be very demanding work.
- While there are lucrative careers in the graphic design field, many job opportunities that offer experience to newcomers and recent graduates can come with relatively low salaries. What are your pay expectations, now and in the future?

Thinking deeply about these questions and answering them honestly will help make your career goals clearer and guide you in knowing which steps you will need to take to get there.

> "Make sure you have a decent idea of what this career is and have some acumen for it. To see if you like it, try using Adobe software at school. Do yearbook or newspaper at school. Dip your toe and see if you like it. Look all around you—anything you see that's printed or online is graphic design. Be aware that it's not always just about being creative. It takes creativity, but that's not all it takes."—Danielle Foster

You are on a fact-finding mission of sorts. A career fact-finding plan, no matter what the field, should include these main steps:

- Find out about educational requirements and schooling expectations. Will you be able to meet any rigorous requirements? This chapter will help you understand the educational paths.
- Seek out opportunities to volunteer or shadow someone doing the job. This will enable you to experience in person what the atmosphere is like, what a typical workday entails, how coworkers interact with each other and with management, and whether you can see yourself thriving in that role and work culture. Use your critical-thinking skills to ask questions and consider whether this is the right environment for you.
- Look into student aid, grants, scholarships, and other ways you can get help to pay for schooling.
- Build a timetable for taking required exams such as the SAT and ACT, applying to schools, visiting schools, and making your decision. You

should write down all important deadlines and have them at the ready when you need them.

- Continue to look for employment that matters during your college years—internships and work experiences that help you get hands-on experience and knowledge about your intended career.
- Talk with professionals working in the job you are considering and ask them what they enjoy about their work, what they find the most challenging, and what path they followed to get there.
- Find a mentor in the field who is interested in helping you. This person can be a great source of information, education, and connections. Don't expect a job (at least not at first); just build a relationship with someone who wants to pass along his or her wisdom and experience. Coffee meetings or even e-mails are a great way to start.

A mentor can help you in many ways. ©valentinrussanov/E+/Getty Images

Where to Go for Help

If you aren't sure where to start, your local library, school library, and guidance counselor's office are great places to begin. Search your local or school library for resources about finding a career path and finding the right schooling that fits your needs and budget. Make an appointment with or e-mail a counselor to ask about taking career interest questionnaires. With a little prodding, you'll be directed to lots of good information online and elsewhere. You can start your research with these sites:

- The Bureau of Labor Statistics' Career Outlook site at www.bls.gov/careeroutlook/home.htm. The US Department of Labor's Bureau of Labor Statistics site doesn't just track job statistics, as you learned in chapter 1. An entire section of the BLS website is dedicated to helping young adults looking to uncover their interests and to match those interests with jobs currently in the market. Check out the section called "Career Planning for High Schoolers." Information is updated based on career trends and jobs in demand, so you'll get practical information as well.

- The Mapping Your Future site at www.mappingyourfuture.org. This site helps you determine a career path and then helps you map out a plan to reach those goals. It includes tips on preparing for college, paying for college, job hunting, résumé writing, and more.

- The Education Planner site at www.educationplanner.org. With separate sections for students, parents, and counselors, this site breaks down the task of planning your career goals into simple, easy-to-understand steps. You can find personality assessments, get tips on preparing for school, read Q&As from counselors, download and use a planner worksheet, read about how to finance your education, and more.

- The TeenLife site at www.teenlife.com. Calling itself "the leading source for college preparation," this site includes lots of information about summer programs, gap year programs, community service, and more. Promoting the belief that spending time out "in the world" outside of the classroom can help students do better in school, find a better fit in terms of career, and even interview better with colleges, this site contains lots of links to volunteer and summer programs.

- The Princeton Review website has a career quiz that focuses on personal interests at www.princetonreview.com/quiz/career-quiz.
- You can find a career test designed to help you find the job of your dreams at www.educations.com/career-test.

Use these sites as jumping-off points and don't be afraid to reach out to real people, such as a guidance counselor or your favorite teacher, for more assistance.

The process of deciding on and planning a career path is daunting. In many ways, the range of choices of careers available today is a wonderful thing. It allows us to refine our career goals and customize them to our own lives and personalities. In other ways, though, too much choice can be extremely daunting, and require a lot of soul-searching to navigate clearly.

Young adults with disabilities can face additional challenges when planning a career path. DO-IT (Disabilities, Opportunities, Internetworking, and Technology) is an organization dedicated to promoting career and education inclusion for everyone. Its website contains a wealth of information and tools to help all young people plan a career path, including self-assessment tests and career exploration questionnaires.

KIM KULTGEN: THE LOVE OF CREATIVITY

Kim Kultgen. *Courtesy of Kim Kultgen*

Kim Kultgen received her bachelor's degree in visual communications design from Purdue University and then got her MBA from Butler University. Her first job out of college was for the American Camping Association, where she worked for two years. She learned hands-on pasteup production and printing there. Things changed a few years after she got out of college, when people began using the computer and creating digital productions.

She worked at Butler University for eight years—two as a graphic designer and six as the

art director. She worked about sixty hours a week. Once she started having chil-
dren, she wanted a position that wasn't as demanding, so she took a job at an
architecture firm as a graphic designer, where she could work forty-hour weeks. She
was there for seven years, then worked as a freelancer for about six years.

When the recession hit, she felt that she needed more reliable income. She
then found her current job at Wood Turningz, where she has spent nine years as a
graphic designer. The company, which is targeted toward hobbyist woodworkers,
sells exotic woods and plastics to make pens, Christmas ornaments, and so on.

Can you explain how you became interested in graphic design?

I started off in college studying computer science and quickly realized I didn't want
to do programming. At the time, my cousin was doing graphic design and I found
it interesting. I was always very artistic. I went back to Purdue that semester and
talked to a counselor. She helped me switch to visual communications design and
I never looked back.

Can you talk about your current position?

I design a weekly e-mail sale and a catalog that promotes all our products. I also
take the photographs (I have a photography minor) and edit and design the website
(make sure it's all up to date). I do design the website but someone else does the
programming. I create postcards, mailers, brochures, and promotions too.

Do you think education prepared you for your job?

I would say yes, although the industry changed so drastically right after I graduated.
If someone went to school now, it would be better. I came out without any computer
knowledge because they just weren't being used yet, and then within a few years
it was all computers. I learned the basic principles of graphic design, which I still
use daily.

What's the best part of being a graphic artist?

I love the creativity. I love Photoshop and I love the creativity that it offers. Also, the
profession is really flexible and you can work out of your home. You are creative as
well as drum up business. It's fairly versatile. If you don't like the subject matter, you
can find something else.

What are some things in this profession that are especially challenging?

You really have to keep up with the technology. You can't really walk away and
jump back in because everything changes constantly. It's hard to leave and then
jump back in easily. You have to stay up to date.

You have to be able to work under pressure. There are a lot of deadlines, and it can be stressful. Also, I work a lot of hours and the compensation isn't as good as I would like.

What are some characteristics of a good graphic designer?

You have to wear a lot of hats. Creative people aren't necessarily drawn to writing code, for example, but you might have to do it all. The evolution of it means you do write code and need a lot of knowledge about lots of technical things too. You need flexibility and need to be able to constantly learn and adapt. It's good to be a self-starter and learn new programs constantly.

Also, time management is huge. There are constant deadlines, so you have to handle the stress properly. Especially if you work for an ad agency—it's really stressful.

What advice do you have for young people considering this career?

I tell people that I went into this career because I love it and wanted to do it. It's not something to do if you're money driven. Some people can make good money, but the majority won't get rich. Go into it because you have a love for the art and want a creative career.

How can a young person prepare for a career in graphic design while in high school?

Working on the high school yearbook or newspaper is a good place to start. Take photography classes at school also. Take whatever art classes are available. Computer training is a big one. Make sure you know the computer programs that are being used in your industry. Adobe is the thing right now. I used all Adobe software. Microsoft products too. You should have decent drawing skills to be able to sketch out ideas, so take drawing classes.

You could also approach companies you know that have in-house design and ask them if you can job shadow or be an assistant. Not to get paid but to learn something. You can get experience by observing. Go to printers, for example—they do a lot of in-house design. Newspapers and book publishers too. You can get knowledge of the production end. Kids now have lots of web training but don't have a good understanding of the production of print materials.

Go observe or shadow wherever you can, if possible.

Any last thoughts?

My first job was working for a not-for-profit, which was a nice environment to learn in. Ad agencies are more cutthroat. Maybe you should know which kind of business you want to work for and find one that matches your personality. In-house design houses and not-for-profits are pleasant places to work. I didn't really like being by myself. Especially in the beginning, you need people to mentor you. It's fun to work with a team and brainstorm with them. And that helps you grow in your career. So don't start as a freelancer or be the only one on staff, at least at the start of your career. You'll learn much more working with a team of designers.

Making High School Count

Regardless of the career you choose, there are some basic yet important things you can do while in high school to position yourself in the most advantageous way. Remember—it's not just about having the best application, it's also about figuring out which areas of graphic design you actually would enjoy and which ones don't suit you.

- Work on your portfolio. Don't wait until you can be paid professionally to start building a body of work, be it icon art, design ideas, sample web pages, computer-generated images, or layout spreads. Hone your skills as much as you can.
- Hone your communication skills in English, speech, and debate. You'll need excellent communication skills in a job where you'll have to speak with everyone from coworkers to clients to bosses.
- Become comfortable using all kinds of computer software.
- Volunteer in as many settings as you can. Read on to learn more about this important aspect of career planning.
- Take online courses in HTML, CCS, JavaScript, the Adobe suite (Photoshop, Illustrator, InDesign, and Acrobat), and so on. You can find relatively inexpensive courses online and gain access to things like Photoshop at a reduced student rate (or use the versions at your high school).

Courses to Take in High School

Depending on your high school and what courses you have access to, there are many subjects that will help you prepare for a career in graphic design. If you go to a school that offers programming and multimedia courses, that's a good place to start. However, there are other courses and subjects that are just as relevant. Some of them may seem unrelated initially, but they will all help you prepare yourself and develop key skills.

- *Language arts.* Because team collaboration is the essence of a job in the graphic design industry, ensuring you know how to communicate clearly and effectively—both in spoken and written language—will be key. It helps avoid unnecessary frustration, delays, financial and time costs, and errors if you can clearly convey and understand ideas.
- *Math.* If you are aiming to be an artist in the graphic design industry, you may not think math is that important. However, computers have changed how multimedia artists need to think. Need to make shapes in Illustrator using Bezier curves? Should probably take some math courses. And if you aim to own your own business, math is definitely essential for working with budgets and managing profits and losses, among other tasks.
- *Interpersonal communication/public speaking.* These courses will be an asset in any profession, including the graphic design industry. If you need to present ideas to your team, to sales staff, to clients—these will be very important skills to hone.
- *Business and economics.* As with any type of business, if you have the ambition to run your own, knowledge gained in business and economics classes will prepare you to make smarter business and financial decisions.
- *Specialized software.* Graphic designers and multimedia artists will need to be skilled in the technical tools they will use daily in their work. This could include HTML, CSS, JavaScript, and the Adobe suite, as well as any multimedia apps and programs.

Gaining Work Experience

The best way to learn anything is to do it. When it comes to preparing for a career in the graphic design industry, there are several options for gaining real-world experience and getting a feel for whether you are choosing the right career for you.

The one big benefit of jobs in the graphic design industry is you don't have to land a work-experience opportunity at an established or upcoming company to prove what you've got and what you can do. Rather than wait for someone to invite you to work for them, you are wise to keep working on your own, to show not only your talent but your passion.

This means that if you want to create graphic designs for websites, for example, create some on your own and create a strong portfolio. If you are a strong artist in another context or medium, be sure to create works that are suitable to the market you want to get into.

TIPS FROM THE EXPERTS: CREATING A STANDOUT PORTFOLIO

There are many online tools available—free and by subscription—that help you create a portfolio of your artwork. Your portfolio is an important part of your application, as it allows you not only to showcase your work but to express who you are and how passionate you are about what you do. Your résumé is important, but your portfolio is where you really show your talent and your personal style.

Here are some of the main takeaways about creating your portfolio:

- Create your portfolio online and always keep your portfolio site up to date.
- Think about your audience when creating your portfolio.
- Don't distract from the work. Make your presentation about the work, not the interface.
- The fewer clicks it takes before your work is presented, the better.
- Make sure your images are relevant to the job you are applying for and don't be afraid to shuffle them to fit.
- Keep in mind that whichever platform you choose should be as customizable as possible so that you can keep your creative flow and stick to your brand.

- Make it easy to find you. Your contact info should be easily accessible from any point on your webpage.
- Never stop creating. Revamp your site design every so often. Try to post something new as often as you can.
- Don't include anything but your very best work. Better a few pieces that rock than a wide variety of samples that make your work quality look variable.
- Most important: Always push yourself, and get critique and feedback from the most critical person you know.[1]

Come up with concepts that are related to the kind of graphic design you want to do. If you want to get into packaging design, create some stellar designs for product packaging. If you want to do web and mobile design, create websites that work well on phones as well. You don't need to have an official internship or job placement to gain experience. You can impress potential employers—or college entrance boards, if you're still in high school—with your own ideas from your portfolio.

Beyond showing off your skills, it's crucial to work on your own to develop websites, logos, artwork, GIFs, or whatever for the career you want to pursue. This will prove your passion for your specific area of graphic design and the way in which you want to bring your skill set to graphic design in particular.

Educational Requirements

Depending on the type of job you want to pursue in the graphic design industry, various levels of education are required. In some cases, it is possible to enter the field without a college degree—but in order to advance to higher levels within your career, a degree is usually preferred by employers. The following outlines the general requirements in terms of education for different graphic design jobs.

Later in this chapter, you will learn about some considerations to keep in mind when deciding what level of education is best for you to pursue. Chapter

3 outlines in more detail the types of programs offered should you want to pursue post–high school training and certification or an associate's, bachelor's, or master's degree.

- *Multimedia artist/animator (including logo design):* A bachelor's degree in computer graphics, fine arts, or a related field and a strong portfolio is your best bet. Multimedia artists are expected to be proficient in tools such as Adobe Photoshop, Illustrator, Flash, and Maya, as well as JavaScript.[2]
- *Web/mobile designer:* Education ranges from a high school diploma to a bachelor's degree. An associate's degree in web design or related field is the most common requirement. Others have a bachelor's degree in computer science or programming. Knowledge of computer programming languages such as JavaScript, HTML, CSS, Java, and Python, are also required.[3]
- *Graphic designer (including packaging design):* An associate's or bachelor's degree in graphic design, art, or a related field and a strong portfolio is your best course of action.[4]

WHY CHOOSE AN ASSOCIATE'S DEGREE?

With a two-year degree—called an associate's degree—you are qualified to apply for certain positions within the graphic design field. Common associate's degrees offered that pertain to graphic design are in computer graphics, web design, programming, graphic design, and animation.

These degree programs are sufficient to give you a knowledge base to begin your career and can serve as a basis should you decide to pursue a four-year degree later. Do keep in mind, though, that all jobs within the graphic design industry are quite competitive. If you are prepared to put in the financial and time commitment to earn an associate's degree and are sure of the career goal you have set for yourself, consider earning a bachelor's. With so much competition out there, the more of an edge you can give yourself, the better your chances will be.

Keep in mind that community colleges and technical schools can be a much cheaper way (as much as half the cost) to earn the same degree, and as long as those programs are accredited, it won't matter to potential employers that you didn't attend a more well-known university.

WHY CHOOSE A BACHELOR'S DEGREE?

A bachelor's degree—which usually takes four years to obtain—is a requirement for most careers related to the graphic design industry. In general, the higher education you pursue, the better your odds are to advance in your career, which means more opportunity and often more compensation.

The difference between an associate's and a bachelor's degree is, of course, the amount of time each takes to complete. To earn a bachelor's degree, a candidate must complete forty college credits, compared with twenty for an associate's. This translates to more courses completed and a deeper exploration of degree content, even though similar content is covered in both.

Even when not required, a bachelor's degree can help advance your career, give you an edge over the competition in the field, and earn you a higher starting salary than holders of an associate's degree.

In addition to deciding how long you should go to school, another important conclusion to come to is whether you consider yourself an artist who will learn the programs and applications needed to be artistic or a technical person who wants to use technology to create things and be creative. This isn't a subtle difference when it comes to the career trajectory.

Choosing the Creative Path

If you have the drive and talent to pursue a career as an artist, a bachelor's degree in fine arts or graphic design may be the best path for you. Then you will need to learn the programs and applications you need to be computer literate in your field. There are hundreds of postsecondary colleges, universities, and independent institutes in the United States with programs in art and design. These programs include classes in fine art, principles of design, computerized design, commercial graphics production, printing techniques, and website design.[5]

Many bachelor's degree programs require students to complete a year of basic art and design courses before being admitted to a formal degree program. Some schools require applicants to submit sketches and other examples of their artistic ability, in the form of a portfolio.

Choosing the Technical Path

Another way to approach the field of graphic design is from the computer science angle. Programs in computer graphics often include courses in computer science in addition to art courses. If you know for sure that you want to be a multimedia artist or a website/mobile designer, having the technical education can be an asset. You still need to create unique ideas and projects, but those skills can be honed specifically for the kind of job you want.

Your graphic design education will be a hands-on, collaborative experience. ©nd3000/iStock/Getty Images Plus

Which path you take depends on your talents, your focus, and your ultimate career plans. You may find that you are initially more marketable if you get a computer graphics–related degree, but you might have to work harder to make sure you aren't pigeonholed into a technical job where you don't get to express your creativity. If you get a degree in art and design and you have the technical know-how, you have a better chance at being hired for your creative talents to begin with. But keep in mind that it's a highly competitive market to break into.

No matter the path you choose, make sure the university or college you attend is properly accredited so that your degree will mean something to employers out in the real world.

WHAT'S THE DIFFERENCE BETWEEN ACCREDITATION AND CERTIFICATION?

The terms *accreditation* and *certification* can be confusing, and people often mix them up and use them incorrectly, contributing to the overall confusion. Accreditation is the act of officially recognizing an organizational body, person, or educational facility as having a particular status or being qualified to perform a particular activity; for example, schools and colleges are accredited. The National Association of Schools of Art and Design (https://nasad.arts-accredit.org), founded in 1944, is an accrediting organization of colleges, schools, and universities in the United States.

Certification, on the other hand, is the process of confirming that a person has certain skills or knowledge. This is usually provided by some third-party review, assessment, or educational body. Individuals, not organizations, are certified. This also might be referred to as being licensed. Certification programs are generally available through software product vendors, such as Adobe. Such certifications can give you a competitive advantage over your peers.

Experience-Related Requirements

There are many ways you can gain helpful experience in the graphic design field before and during the time you're pursuing your education. This can and should start in high school, especially during the summers. Experience is important for many reasons:

- You need to start building that all-important portfolio.
- Shadowing others in the profession can help reveal what the job is really like and whether it's something that you think you want to do, day in and day out. This is a relatively risk-free way to explore different career paths. Ask any seasoned adult and he or she will tell you that figuring out what you *don't* want to do is sometimes more important than figuring out what you *do* want to do.
- Internships and volunteer work are a relatively quick way to gain work experience and develop job skills.
- Volunteering can help you learn the intricacies of the profession, such as what types of environments are best and which skills you need to work on.
- Gaining experience during your high school years sets you apart from the many others who are applying to postsecondary programs.
- Volunteering in the field means that you'll be meeting many others doing the job that you might someday want to do (think: career networking). You have the potential to develop mentor relationships, cultivate future job prospects, and get to know people who can recommend you for later positions. Studies show that about 85 percent of jobs are found through personal contacts.[6]

"Try to get into a company to shadow or intern, even just to make copies. Get in so you hear the lingo and see how the profession really works."—Chris Shute, creative director

---

Consider these tidbits of advice to maximize your volunteer experience. They will help you stand out:

- Get diverse experiences. For example, try to shadow in at least two different places of business.

- Try to gain forty hours of volunteer experience in each setting. This is typically considered enough to show that you understand what a full work week looks like in that setting. This can be as few as four to five hours per week over ten weeks or so.
- Don't be afraid to ask questions. Just be considerate of others' time and wait until they are not busy to pursue your questions. Asking good questions shows that you have a real curiosity for the profession.
- Maintain and cultivate professional relationships. Write thank-you notes, send updates about your application progress and tell them where you decide to go to school, and check in occasionally. If you want to find a good mentor, you need to be a gracious and willing mentee.[7]

Look at these kinds of experiences as ways to learn about the profession, show people how capable you are, and make connections with others that could last your career. It may even help you to get into the college of your choice, and it will definitely help you write your personal statement that explains why you want to work in graphic design.

Another way to find a position—or at least a company that is open to curious students—is to start with your high school guidance counselor or website and visit the websites listed in this book. Also, don't be afraid to just pick up the phone and call local companies. Be prepared to start by making copies, assisting with clerical work, and other such tasks. Being on-site, no matter what you're doing, will teach you more than you know. With a great attitude and work ethic, you will likely be given more responsibility over time.

Networking

Because it's so important, another last word about networking: It's important to develop mentor relationships even at this stage. Remember that about 85 percent of jobs are found through personal contacts. If you know someone in the field, don't hesitate to reach out. Be patient and polite, but ask for help, perspective, and guidance.

"Don't be afraid to talk to people and network for jobs and connections! I wish I would have done more of that in my early days."—Shawn Morningstar, graphic designer

If you don't know anyone, ask your school guidance counselor to help you make connections. Or pick up the phone yourself. Reaching out with a genuine interest in knowledge and a real curiosity about the field will go a long way. You don't need a job or an internship just yet—just a connection that could blossom into a mentoring relationship. Follow these important but simple rules for the best results when networking:

- Do your homework about a potential contact, connection, university, school, or employer before you make contact. Be sure to have a general understanding of what they do and why. But don't be a know-it-all. Be open and ready to ask good questions.

Making connections with others in your prospective field is a great way to learn and be exposed to opportunity. ©izusek/E+/Getty Images

- Be considerate of professionals' time and resources. Think about what they can get from you in return for mentoring or helping you.
- Speak and write using proper English. Proofread all your letters, e-mails, and even texts. Think about how you will be perceived at all times.
- Always stay positive.
- Show your passion for the subject matter.

Don't forget that your high school guidance counselor can be a great source of information and connections.

Summary

In this chapter, you learned even more about what it's like to be a graphic artist and designer. This chapter discussed the educational requirements of these different areas of multimedia and graphic design. You also learned about getting experience and creating your portfolio. At this time, you should have a good idea of the schooling options and the requirements needed to start creating your portfolio. You hopefully even contemplated some questions about what kind of educational path fits your strengths, time requirements, and wallet. Are you starting to picture your career plan? If not, that's okay, as there's still time.

Remember that no matter which of these areas of graphic design you pursue, you must maintain your knowledge of the latest and greatest computer programs, applications, and programming languages used in your field. Advances in technology are frequent and constant, and it's vitally important that you keep apprised of what's happening in your field. The bottom line is that you need to have a lifelong love of learning to succeed in any computer field.

Chapter 3 goes into a lot more detail about pursuing the best educational path. The chapter covers how to find the best value for your education and includes discussion about financial aid and scholarships. At the end of chapter 3, you should have a much clearer view of the educational landscape and how and where you fit in.

3

Pursuing the Education Path

When it comes time to start looking at colleges, universities, or postsecondary schools, many high schoolers tend to freeze up at the enormity of the job ahead of them. This chapter will help break down this process for you so it won't seem so daunting.

Finding the right college or learning institution is important, and it's a big step toward achieving your career goals and dreams. The last chapter covered the various educational requirements of these professions, which means you should now be ready to find the right institution of learning. This isn't always just about finding the very best school that you can afford and are accepted into, although that might end up being your path. It should also be about finding the right fit so that you can have the best possible experience during your post–high school years.

But the truth is that attending postsecondary schooling isn't just about getting a degree. It's also about learning how to be an adult, managing your life and your responsibilities, being exposed to new experiences, growing as a person, and otherwise moving toward becoming an adult who contributes to society. College offers you an opportunity to become an interesting person with perspective on the world and empathy and consideration for people other than yourself, if you let it.

An important component of how successful you will be in college is finding the right fit, the right school that brings out the best in you and challenges you at different levels. I know—no pressure, right? Just as with finding the right profession, your ultimate goal should be to match your personal interests, goals, and personality with the college's goals and perspective. For example, small liberal arts colleges have a much different feel and philosophy than Big 10 or Pac-12 state schools. And rest assured that all this advice applies even if you're planning on attending community college or another postsecondary school.

• Don't worry, though: In addition to these soft skills, this chapter does dive into the specifics of how to find a good fit, no matter what you want to do. It also covers what you can do to best prepare for school before you even apply.

Before Graphic Design School

Before you get the point of finding and applying to schools, there is a lot you can do to prepare for a career in multimedia arts or graphic design. The first step is to experience all the design and art you can. Take classes, go to exhibits, peruse great websites, visit museums, look at art books, review print and web advertisements, study product packaging that grabs you, read about artists who interest you in books and online, and even scroll through Instagram.

LEARN ABOUT DESIGN AND ART

While you're still in high school, take all the design and art classes you can. Whatever your school offers, take it. Get to know your teachers and ask them for feedback on your work. How can you make it better? Are there any common mistakes you're making that you could fix? Do they notice anything about the work that makes it special? Even if a particular teacher doesn't have good answers for these questions, it's good to get in the mindset of asking them. Be respectful and polite, and consider what you're being told even if it doesn't make sense to you at the time. It might become clear later on. Also, your teachers are the first people you'll want to ask for school recommendations.

In addition to school classes—or if you don't have access to art and design classes in school—seek out community classes. These are usually taught by professional artists who know a lot about their own medium. This is an opportunity to take classes that aren't offered at your school, or to go deeper in a medium that speaks to you.

Many high schools offer classes like:

- Web design
- Multimedia design
- Drawing
- Graphic design

- Painting
- Photography

Community design and art classes are often offered by local nonprofit arts centers in afterschool programs and/or summer camps. Sometimes professional artists and designers will offer classes to individual students or small groups.

SEE DESIGN

A great way to begin learning about good design is to study current designs in the world. The good news is that design is everywhere! Check out magazines, websites, packaging, billboards, brochures, pamphlets, mobile apps, books, and more. Note what works and what doesn't and try to figure out why. Why does one design appeal to you and really pop, where another doesn't seem to convey the right message? Consider fonts, colors, and images as well as the actual words used.

"Always keep your creativity fresh by looking at art, visiting museums, seeing movies, looking at fashion and nature. Develop your own design style and create a powerful portfolio that showcases your design style and talent."—Sue Porritt, graphic designer

Studying art and design is a great way to learn. ©Jupiterimages/DigitalVision/Getty Images

The same goes with art. If you are lucky enough to have a local art museum or two, go again and again. Look at all the collections—even if you're not sure what the appeal is—and spend some time with your favorite pieces. Consider the use of light, color, materials, space, and overall feel.

SHAWN MORNINGSTAR: DESIGNER FROM THE START

Shawn Morningstar's design career started in earnest when she was fifteen, when her father had a custom fireplace company and her mom worked at Apple. She created a brochure for her dad's company, and her dad had it copied. She had a computer before any of her friends did because her mom worked at Apple. People would ask her to help make their papers look pretty. In the summers, she worked at Apple as a writer's assistant. She did formatting in Word and took freelance work incorporating edits at Apple. Her mom worked in publishing, and she got used to the software. She got her bachelor's degree in communications and was planning to be a broadcast journalist.

Shawn Morningstar. *Courtesy of Shawn Morningstar*

She took a few design classes after she graduated and started working at Apple doing graphic design. The gig at Apple was awesome; she worked there for more than five years after graduation. She was also getting freelance layout jobs, and during that time Apple was experiencing layoffs. She decided to leave the company and went out on her own as a freelancer in 1995. She had so much work—mostly in print publishing—that she couldn't handle it. It freed her up to work and live wherever she wanted.

Can you explain how you became interested in graphic design?

I have always liked putting things together on a page in a creative way. I have always been visual and enjoy art, but I don't consider myself a fine artist. When I was at Apple, I saw someone doing the job of book designer and I thought that was a neat job.

Can you talk about your current position?

Things really slowed down in print publishing a few years ago. I work now as a legal assistant two days a week and actually use my graphic design skills there. I have a few freelance design projects here and there as well. I don't really advertise anymore, but people I've worked with do come back through my life now and then. I feel lucky that I got to do books and focus on that. I got really good at it. But it just went away pretty much, which is frustrating. Doing ads and brochures is more creative but it's not my best skill.

What's the best part of being a graphic designer?

For me, it's all about the flexible hours, as I worked freelance. When I had my kids, I could work when the kids were at school and when they were sleeping, which was great. When my husband got laid off, I was able to take on much, much more and worked sixteen-hour days. It really helped and kept our life and house going.

I also like having piecemeal projects. You're really busy and then you have down time. It's not the same thing every day. It's always different. There's a lot of change. Also, the harder I worked, the more I made.

What are some things in this profession that are especially challenging right now?

Outsourcing is a big problem for American workers. And the results look horrible, in my opinion. Is that the future of publishing? Everybody and their uncle "knows" graphic design now, so people think they can do it themselves on their own computers. People with no experience can do it for super cheap and you're competing with them.

What are some characteristics of a good graphic designer?

You need to be someone who can deal with a lot of change. You can't be married to your design. You have to be ready for criticism and can't take the feedback personally. You should expect that you'll get feedback. This is how you learn. Be flexible and open-minded.

If you want to be freelance, you really have to be able to deal effectively with deadlines because people are counting on you. You need a good eye for design. I like it simple and clean and open and consistent.

What advice do you have for young people considering this career?

Maybe put a portfolio together showing bad design in real life and show how you would do it better. Get a website for sure. Go to the sites where you can bid on projects. Work for charities. Do the newsletter and such. This teaches you about design principles, making things fit, and making it look good. That will give you real-world experience.

Print everything out, because it looks different on-screen than when you print it. Make it fit into the paradigm in which it will appear. It will show you what it really looks like.

Don't be afraid to talk to people and network for jobs and connections. Get the best equipment you can early on. You can use the school's equipment, but strive for the best you have access to.

How can a young person prepare for a career in graphic design while in high school?
Work on the high school yearbook or school newspaper. See if you can design flyers for the band, theater troupe, etc. I used to go to Barnes & Noble and spend hours and hours looking at what looks good and what doesn't. There are also great design books out there. Read lots of books, magazines, websites, and so on. See what you like and don't like.

Any last thoughts?
If anybody tells you you can't make a living at being an artist, don't listen. That's not true. You just have to try hard and not give up!

DESIGN THINGS

You do this already, right? Otherwise you wouldn't be wondering if a graphic design degree is right for you. So keep it up! Don't limit yourself to class assignments. Make what *you* want to make too.

Keep a sketchbook. It's a great place to make those all-important observational drawings, as well as planning your personal work and making notes on designs that occur to you. Keep your sketchbook with you so you can use it whenever inspiration strikes.

The work you do before applying to school will make up the portfolio you use to apply. Keep track of all your best ideas and designs and be sure to have excellent digital images of them made.

CREATING A PORTFOLIO

Your portfolio is a showcase of all your best work. At different times in your life, it will contain different types of work depending on what you're using it for. If you are applying to design school, your portfolio should be a broad representation of your best work in the various media you use.

So what should your portfolio contain? Different schools will have some different requirements, but in general you want to showcase:

- Ten to twenty examples of your absolute best work—think of your portfolio as your greatest hits
- Variety—showcase the different media you work in
- Personal work—pieces that come from your life or experiences in a way that's meaningful to you
- Your most original work—show your ideas and what you will bring to the experience
- Anything else a specific school has asked you to include, such as your sketchbook[1]

Your portfolio should mostly consist of finished work. Make sure your site is clean and easy to navigate. Don't make people dig through the site to find your work. Search the web for "graphic design portfolios" for inspiring examples. Chapter 4 goes into more detail about building and maintaining a great portfolio. Also consider whether you need a physical portfolio for in-person interviews—especially if you're a print designer, you should think about creating a physical version.

HANDLING CRITIQUE

Design critiques take some students by surprise. You hear the word *critique* and it sounds like criticism—like listing what's wrong with you and your work. But in an art or design class, critique is an essential, objective process of analyzing and evaluating each student's work. It's not about you as a person; it's about your work and development as a designer.

The purpose of critique is to help you learn more about how others see your work, how to work together as a supportive group, and how to offer your opinion in a useful and meaningful way.

During a class critique, it's important to show respect to the other students as well as the teacher by following the etiquette of critiques.

When Your Work Is Being Critiqued

- Listen. Don't interrupt or argue
- Keep an open mind. Even if the comments you receive seem off-base, take them in and consider them. They might turn out to be very valuable.
- Remember that what you hear is not meant as a personal attack; it's meant to be helpful.
- Restate what you hear to be sure you understand.

When You're Critiquing Others

- Be polite. Remember how you feel when it's your turn.
- Keep your comments about the work, not the designer.
- Stay objective. Focus on the elements of the piece, even if you don't like the style or genre.
- Avoid making value judgments (good, bad, beautiful, ugly, decorative, derivative).
- Be specific with your suggestions and keep them focused on ways to improve the piece.
- Offer helpful suggestions to everyone. Don't tell your friends their work is perfect and run down everyone else.

Now that you have some idea about what you can do before it's time to apply to schools, let's move next to finding the right educational fit for your needs.

Finding a School That Fits Your Personality

Before looking at the details of good schools for graphic design, it will behoove you to take some time to consider what type of school will be best for you. Answering questions like the ones that follow can help you narrow your search and focus on a smaller set of choices. Write your answers to these questions down somewhere where you can refer to them often, such as in the Notes app on your phone.

- *Size:* Does the size of the school matter to you? Colleges and universities range in size from five hundred or fewer students to twenty-five thousand students.
- *Community location:* Would you prefer to be in a rural area, a small town, a suburban area, or a large city? How important is the location of the school in the larger world?
- *Distance from home:* How far away from home—in terms of hours or miles away—do you want/are you willing to go? Can you drive or will you need to fly home?
- *Housing options:* What kind of housing would you prefer? Dorms, off-campus apartments, and private homes are all common options.
- *Student body:* How would you like the student body to look? Think about coed versus all-male and all-female settings, as well as ethnic and racial diversity, how many students are part-time versus full-time, and the percentage of commuter students.
- *Academic environment:* Which majors are offered, and at which degree levels? Research the student-faculty ratio. Are the classes taught often by actual professors or more often by the teaching assistants? How many internships does the school typically provides to students? Are independent study or study abroad programs available in your area of interest?
- *Financial aid availability/cost:* Does the school provide ample opportunities for scholarships, grants, work-study programs, and the like? Does cost play a role in your options? (For most people, it does.)
- *Support services:* How strong are the school's academic and career placement counseling services?
- *Social activities and athletics:* Does the school offer clubs that you are interested in? Which sports are offered? Are scholarships available?
- *Specialized programs:* Does the school offer honors programs or programs for veterans or students with disabilities or special needs?

Not all of these questions are going to be important to you, and that's fine. Be sure to make note of aspects that don't matter as much to you. You might change your mind as you visit colleges, but it's important to make note of where you are to begin with.

MAKE THE MOST OF SCHOOL VISITS

If it's at all practical and feasible, you should visit the schools you're considering. To get a real feel for any college or school, you need to walk around the campus and buildings, spend some time in the common areas where students hang out, and sit in on a few classes. You can also sign up for campus tours, which are typically given by current students. This is another good way to see the school and ask questions of someone who knows. Be sure to visit the specific school/building that covers your intended major as well. Websites and brochures won't be able to convey that intangible feeling you'll get from a visit.

Make a list of questions that are important to you before you visit. In addition to the questions listed earlier in this chapter, consider these questions as well:

- What is the makeup of the current freshman class? Is the campus diverse?
- What is the meal plan like? What are the food options?
- Where do most of the students hang out between classes? (Be sure to visit this area.)
- How long does it take to walk from one end of the campus to the other?
- What types of transportation are available for students? Does campus security provide escorts to cars, dorms, and other on-campus destinations at night?

In order to be ready for your visit and make the most of it, consider these tips and words of advice:

- Be sure to do some research. At the very least, spend some time on the college's website. You may find your questions are addressed adequately there.
- Make a list of questions.
- Arrange to meet with a professor in your area of interest or to visit the specific school.
- Be prepared to answer questions about yourself and why you are interested in this school.
- Dress in neat, clean, and casual clothes. Avoid overly wrinkled clothing or anything with stains.
- Listen and take notes.
- Don't interrupt.

- Be positive and energetic.
- Make eye contact when someone speaks directly to you.
- Ask questions.
- Thank people for their time.

Finally, be sure to send thank-you notes or e-mails after the visit is over. Remind recipients when you visited the campus and thank them for their time.

U.S. News & World Report puts it best when it reports that the college that fits you best is one that:

- Offers a degree that matches your interests and needs
- Provides a style of instruction that matches the way you like to learn
- Provides a level of academic rigor to match your aptitude and preparation
- Offers a community that feels like home to you
- Values you for what you do well[2]

Take some time to find the right academic fit; it's worth it. ©Drazen/E+/Getty Images

According to the National Center for Educational Statistics, which is part of the US Department of Education, six years after entering college for an undergraduate degree, only 59 percent of students have graduated.[3] Barely half of those students will graduate from college in their lifetime.[4]

Hopefully, this section has impressed upon you the importance of finding the right college fit. Take some time to paint a mental picture of the kind of university or school setting that will best complement your needs. Then read on for specifics about degrees.

Determining Your Degree Plan

There are many options when it comes to pursing an education in the graphic design or multimedia arts field. These include vocational schools, two-year community colleges, and four-year colleges. This section will help you select the track that is most suited to you.

WHAT IS A GAP YEAR?

Taking a year off between high school and college, often called a gap year, is normal, perfectly acceptable, and almost required in many countries around the world. It is becoming increasingly acceptable in the United States as well. Even Malia Obama, President Obama's daughter, did it. Because the cost of college has gone up dramatically, it literally pays for you to know going in what you want to study, and a gap year—well spent—can do lots to help you answer that question.

Some great ways to spend your gap year include joining organizations such as the Peace Corps or AmeriCorps, enrolling in a mountaineering program or other gap year–styled program, backpacking across Europe or other countries on the cheap (be safe and bring a friend), finding a volunteer organization that furthers a cause you believe in or that complements your career aspirations, joining a Road Scholar program (see www.roadscholar.org), teaching English in another country (more information is available at www.gooverseas.com/blog/best-countries-for-seniors-to-teach-english-abroad), or working and earning money for college!

Many students will find that they get much more out of college when they have a year to mature and to experience the real world. The American Gap Year Association reports from alumni surveys that students who take gap years show greater civic engagement, higher college graduation rates, and higher grade point averages (GPAs) in college.[5]

You can use your gap year to explore and solidify your thoughts and plans about being a graphic designer while adding impressive experiences to your college application. See the association's website at https://gapyearassociation.org for lots of advice and resources if you're considering this potentially life-altering experience.

Whether you are opting for a certificate program or a two-year or four-year degree, you will find many schools that offer a variety of programs with different costs and durations. (In the case of certificate programs, twelve to eighteen months is usually the average for full-time participants to complete the required course load). Because of this, it is important to narrow down your options and compare them closely.

Starting Your College Search

It's a good idea to select roughly five to ten schools in a realistic location (for you) that offer the degree or certification you want to earn. If you are considering online programs, include these in your list. Not every school near you or that you have an initial interest in will offer the program you want, of course, so narrow your choices accordingly. With that said, consider attending a university in your resident state, if possible; this will save you lots of money if you attend a state school. Private institutions don't typically discount resident student tuition costs.

Be sure you research the basic GPA and SAT or ACT requirements of each school as well. Although some community colleges do not require standardized tests for the application process, others do.

For students applying to associate's degree programs or greater, most advisers recommend taking both the ACT and the SAT tests during the spring of their junior year at the latest. (The ACT test is generally considered more heavily weighted in science, so take that into consideration.) You can retake these tests and use your highest score, so be sure to leave time for a retake early in your senior year if needed. You want your best score to be available to all the schools you're applying to by January of your senior year, which will also enable your score to be considered with any scholarship applications. Keep in mind these are general timelines—be sure to check the exact deadlines and calendars of the schools to which you're applying!

Once you have found five to ten schools in a realistic location for you that offer the degree you want to pursue, spend some time on their websites studying the requirements for admission. Important factors in your decision about what schools to apply to should include whether or not you meet the requirements, your chances of getting in (but shoot high!), tuition costs and availability of scholarships and grants, location, and the school's reputation and licensure/graduation rates.

Most colleges and universities will list the average stats for the last class accepted to the program, which will give you a sense of your chances of acceptance.

The importance of these characteristics will depend on your grades and test scores, your financial resources, and other personal factors. You will want to find a university with a good design or computer science program that also matches your academic rigor and practical needs.

Finding the Right School

Finding the university or college that's best for you is going to depend on lots of personal factors, as mentioned in the previous sections. However, you can find

Touring the campus and talking to current students is really helpful. ©DGLimages/ iStock/Getty Images Plus

out a few facts about each school's design or computer science program that you can compare with other schools, such as:

- Is the faculty made up of working or retired design professionals? You'll learn best from those who've actually done it.
- Does the design school teach art too? Art and design are not the same, but they are closely related. You cannot be the best designer, of any type, without having at least basic art skills and knowledge. Subjects and skills like color theory, drawing, art history, composition, and others are the basis of design and help to make design professionals better at what they do.
- Is the school accredited, and by whom? The National Association of Schools of Art and Design is one accrediting organization of colleges, schools, and universities in the United States.
- What is the attrition rate (the number of students who leave the program without graduating)? If this number is particularly high, that tells

you something unflattering about the program or the kinds of students they attract.

- What percentage of last year's graduates are employed in the field? Although this is not always in the school's direct control, it is one factor to consider. As part of their career placement services, the school should help you build your portfolio while you're taking classes.
- How is the school and program you're interested in ranked in the nation? Rankings are not the be-all and end-all but they do tell you what people in the know think about the schools you are considering.

"In my opinion, it's more important now than before to get your four-year [bachelor's] degree. In today's world, you should finish your four-year degree and look into certification programs. Being educated about all things web design is vitally important in being able to be employed."—Jill Flores, graphic designer

These factors, combined with the others mentioned in this chapter, should help you get a holistic view of each college you're considering. In all likelihood, no single factor will determine your best choice. Consider making a grid with all these factors mapped out for each school. Sometimes it's helpful to get everything down on paper and take a look at it all together in one place.

Interviewing

Meeting with a design school or department representative is an important part of the admission process. This is your opportunity to tell the school about yourself as a designer and to talk about your work and why it's important to you. It's also your chance to ask questions about the school that go a little deeper than what you can find out online.

Of course, you'll bring your portfolio and be prepared to talk about the work in it. Also be prepared to talk about:

- Projects you've worked on
- Why these projects were important to you

- How you've developed as a designer so far (classes you've taken, media you've explored, places you've traveled)
- Who your favorite designers are and why
- Why you've chosen this particular school
- What qualities you have as a person, student, and designer that would contribute to the school experience
- What books you've read recently (beyond school assignments)

Choosing a Major

Chapter 2 discussed in some detail how to choose the artistic path or the technical path to design. It basically depends on which kind of design you want to do. A bachelor's degree in graphic design or a related field is a great option. However, people who have a bachelor's degree in another field may complete technical training in graphic design to meet most hiring qualifications. Alternatively, you could earn a degree in computer graphics and work on your creativity from that standpoint. Having a computer graphics degree may make it easier for you to find that first job, but you might have to prove yourself more as an artist in those types of positions. In other words, you might have to work harder to be taken seriously as a creative person.

Regardless of the field of study you choose, you'll need an impressive portfolio of work and strong technical skills to succeed. Certification programs are available through software product vendors such as Adobe. Certification in graphic design software demonstrates competence and may provide you with a competitive advantage.[6]

What's It Going to Cost You?

So, the bottom line: what will your education end up costing you? Of course, this depends on many factors, including the type and length of degree you pursue, where you attend (in-state or not, private or public institution), how much in scholarships or financial aid you're able to obtain, your family or personal income, and many other factors. The College Entrance Examination Board

Table 3.1   Average Yearly Tuition, Fees, Room, and Board for Full-Time Undergraduates

Year	Public 4-Year, In-State	Public 4-Year, Out-of-State	Private Nonprofit
2016–2017	$19,488	Not available	$41,465
2017–2018	$20,050	$25,657	$43,139

Source: National Center for Education Statistics, "Average Undergraduate Tuition and Fees," https://nces.ed.gov/programs/digest/d18/tables/dt18_330.20.asp

tracks and summarizes financial data from colleges and universities all over the United States. (You can find more information at www.collegeboard.org.) A sample of the most recent data is shown in table 3.1.

Keep in mind these are averages and reflect the published prices, not the net prices. If you read data about a particular university or find averages in your particular area of interest, you should assume those numbers are closer to reality than these, as they are more specific. This data helps to show you the ballpark figures.

THE ALL-IMPORTANT NET COST

The actual, final price (or net price) that you'll pay for a specific college is the difference between the published price (tuition and fees) to attend that college and any grants, scholarships, and education tax benefits you receive (money you don't have to pay back). This difference can be significant. According to the College Board, "in 2015–2016, the average published price of in-state tuition and fees for public four-year colleges was about $9,410 [*not* including room and board]. But the average net price of in-state tuition and fees for public four-year colleges was only about $3,980."[7]

Most colleges have net price calculators on their websites. These calculators use the information you enter to come up with a personalized estimate of how much gift aid that particular college may offer you—and consequently what it will really cost you to attend. (The net price is a personal number that varies from student to student. It considers factors like financial need, academic performance, and athletic talent.) The net price is the best number to use when you're comparing the costs of different universities, because it takes into account each school's scholarships and grants, which can vary significantly from school to school. By comparing net prices instead of published prices, you might find out that you can actually afford the school you thought was too expensive!

Generally speaking, there is about a 3 percent annual increase in tuition and associated costs to attend college. In other words, if you are expecting to attend college two years after this data was collected, you need to add approximately 6 percent to these numbers. Keep in mind that this assumes no financial aid or scholarships of any kind (so it's not the net cost).

The next sections discuss finding the most affordable path to get the degree you want. Later in this chapter, you'll also learn how to prime the pumps and get as much money for college as you can.

Financial Aid and Student Loans

Finding the money to attend college—whether a two- or four-year college program, an online program, or a vocational career college—can seem overwhelming. But you can do it if you have a plan before you actually start applying to colleges. If you get into your top-choice university, don't let the sticker price turn you away. Financial aid can come from many different sources, and it's available to cover all different kinds of costs you'll encounter during your years in college, including tuition, fees, books, housing, and food.

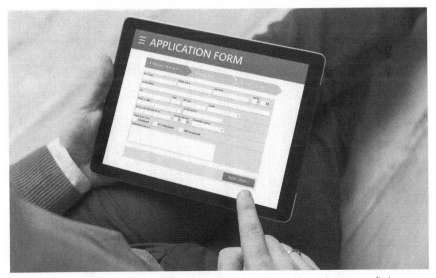

Paying for college can take a creative mix of grants, scholarships, and loans, but you can find your way with some help! ©grinvalds/iStock/Getty Images Plus

The good news is that universities more often offer incentive or tuition discount aid to encourage students to attend. The market is often more competitive in the favor of the student, and colleges and universities are responding by offering more generous aid packages to a wider range of students than they used to. Here are some basic tips and pointers about the financial aid process:

- Apply for financial aid during your senior year. You must fill out the Free Application for Federal Student Aid (FAFSA) form, which can be filed starting October 1 of your senior year until June of the year you graduate.[8] Because the amount of available aid is limited, it's best to apply as soon as you possibly can. See https://studentaid.ed.gov/sa/fafsa to get started.
- Be sure to compare and contrast the deals you get from different schools. There is room to negotiate with universities. The first offer for aid may not be the best you'll get.
- Wait until you receive all offers from your top schools and then use this information to negotiate with your top choice to see if they will match or beat the best aid package you received.
- To be eligible to keep and maintain your financial aid package, you must meet certain grade/GPA requirements. Be sure you are very clear about these academic expectations and keep up with them.
- You must reapply for federal aid every year.
- Look for ways that loans might be deferred or forgiven—service commitment programs are a way to use service to pay back loans.

Watch out for scholarship scams! You should never be asked to pay to submit the FAFSA form (*free* is in its name) or be required to pay a lot to find appropriate aid and scholarships. These are free services. If an organization promises you'll get aid or claims you have to "act now or miss out," these are both warning signs of a less-than-reputable organization. Note that these organizations are not affiliated with or endorsed by the US Department of Education (ED).

You should also be careful with your personal information to avoid identity theft as well. Simple things like closing and exiting your browser after visiting sites where you entered personal information goes a long way. Don't share your student aid ID number with anyone, either.

It's important to understand the different forms of financial aid that are available to you. That way, you'll know how to apply for different kinds and get the best financial aid package that fits your needs and strengths. The two main categories that financial aid falls under are gift aid, which doesn't have to be repaid, and self-help aid, which includes loans that must be repaid and work-study funds that are earned. The next sections cover the various types of financial aid that fit into one of these areas.

GRANTS

Grants typically are awarded to students who have financial need but can also be used in the areas of athletics, academics, demographics, veteran support, and special talents. They do not have to be paid back. Grants can come from federal agencies, state agencies, specific universities, and private organizations. Most federal and state grants are based on financial need.

Examples of grants are the Pell Grant, SMART Grant, and the Federal Supplemental Educational Opportunity Grant. Visit the US Department of Education's Federal Student Aid site at https://studentaid.ed.gov/types/ grants-scholarships for lots of current information about grants.

SCHOLARSHIPS

Scholarships are merit-based aid that does not have to be paid back. They are typically awarded based on academic excellence or some other special talent, such as music or art. Scholarships can also be athletic-based, minority-based, aid for women, and so forth. These are typically not awarded by federal or state governments, but instead come from the specific school you applied to as well as private and nonprofit organizations.

Be sure to reach out directly to the financial aid officers of the schools you want to attend. These people are great contacts who can lead you to many more sources of scholarships and financial aid. Visit GoCollege's Financial Aid Finder at www.gocollege.com/financial-aid/scholarships/types for lots more information about how scholarships in general work.

LOANS

Many types of loans are available especially for students to pay for their post-secondary education. However, the important thing to remember here is that loans must be paid back, with interest. (This is the extra cost of borrowing the money and is usually a percentage of the amount you borrow.) Be sure you understand the interest rate you will be charged. Is this fixed or will it change over time? Are payments on the loan and interest deferred until you graduate (meaning you don't have to begin paying it off until after you graduate)? Is the loan subsidized (meaning the federal government pays the interest until you graduate)? These are all points you need to be clear about before you sign on the dotted line.

There are many types of loans offered to students, including need-based loans, non–need-based loans, state loans, and private loans. Two very reputable federal loans are the Perkins Loan and the Direct Stafford Loan. For more information about student loans, visit https://bigfuture.collegeboard.org/pay-for-college/loans/types-of-college-loans.

FEDERAL WORK-STUDY

The US federal work-study program provides part-time jobs for undergraduate and graduate students with financial need so they can earn money to pay for educational expenses. The focus of such work is on community service work and work related to a student's course of study. Not all schools participate in this program, so be sure to check with the financial aid office at any schools you are considering if this is something you are counting on. The sooner you apply, the more likely you will get the job you desire and be able to benefit from the program, as funds are limited. See https://studentaid.ed.gov/sa/types/work-study for more information about this opportunity.

SUE PORRITT: A SPECIALTY IN CHILDREN'S MAGAZINES

Sue Porritt earned her BFA in Illustration from Parsons School of Design (part of the New School) in New York. She has worked in the design field for about thirty years.

She most recently worked for a children's magazine publisher (Thomas & Friends magazine, Redan Publishing). She was first on staff and then became a freelancer. She has been working as a freelancer for ten years. She primarily does design and illustration work, with a specialty in magazine and book covers.

Can you explain how you became interested in graphic design?

When I was in second grade, we had a project to showcase what job we wanted to do when we grew up. I was always attracted to magazines, so I designed my own magazine with a cover. It was basically a collage of other magazine images with my drawings mixed in. I first felt that spark of interest in illustration and design then. In high school, I took art and photography courses. This was during the analog days. There were no opportunities for digital training then.

Sue Porritt. *Courtesy of Sue Porritt*

Can you talk about your current position?

Finishing up with *Thomas & Friends* magazine at this time. Redan will not be publishing it much longer. I am also freelancing and looking for other publishers. My specialties are children's magazines and licensing.

I design the covers and create the layouts for the magazine. That means I work with editors, art directors, licensors (who own the characters we show), and other freelancers. I am the main designer on the magazine. I also design ads and promotional literature for the magazine. I get to see lots of different ways of working, which was great.

Did your education prepare you for the field?

Yes. My training wasn't digital, and that would have been nice to have, but that wasn't readily available. I learned all that on the job a few years later. However, school did prepare me, and I still use some of the basic things I learned. You learn design principles like typography and the way a page is properly laid out. You learn how to design and create impactful images and covers. My education was about composition and layout, mainly. It helped me develop a thick skin too. All that I learned in college.

What's the best part of being a graphic designer?

The spark of creativity! Getting the brief (description of the project, purpose, size, where it will appear, possible contents, etc.) and coming up with ideas that might fulfill the brief and be successful. There are constraints and you work within those, and it's a great challenge to be creative within that.

What are some things in this profession that are especially challenging right now?

The transition from print to digital has been major in the last few years. Keeping on top of all the digital trends and making sure your creativity works for social media. Younger generations have been born into that paradigm, which is good.

I have been trained for digital and worked extensively in digital, but the technology changes so quickly and you need to keep on top of it. You have to keep your skills up to date, as you would in any other field.

Print is in transition, and it's a challenge. I think there is a home for it, but getting the latest generation to embrace print is a challenge. The future is a question mark. Print can, however, be a break from the never-ending screen time.

What are some characteristics of a good graphic designer?

You need to develop a thick skin and not take criticism and rejection personally. Remove your personal feelings from the equation.

My best training in college was learning how to take criticism well and not be upset when someone didn't like my design. In college, it was a rude awaking, but a good lesson. Your designs can become very personal. It's understandable, because you are putting yourself out there, but you need to work on this.

Other good qualities include being accurate, being nimble with different design ideas, and being original.

What advice do you have for young people considering this career?

Always keep your creativity fresh by looking at art, visiting museums, seeing movies, looking at fashion and nature. Develop your own design style and create a powerful portfolio that showcases your design style and talent.

Stay on top of new design trends and digital programs. Don't be afraid to look for design opportunities in areas you might not expect to find them; you never know. Things come knocking at your door and they might be great opportunities to stretch yourself.

How can a young person prepare for a career in graphic design while in high school?

Develop a strong portfolio, including your own style and a good range of abilities (studio art, digital designed ads, logos, and so on). Have a variety of different strengths. Find mentors who can give you advice on a good portfolio for college.

Look for internships and volunteer work too—at your local newspaper, for example. If you live near an art school, you could find an internship during the summer. It doesn't have to be design specific. Just get exposed to the creative world. You can still hone your visual skills. Just because you aren't creating something, if you are looking and seeing, your creative mind is alive and fresh.

Work on the yearbook or the school newspaper too, if it's available. I was involved in the yearbook at school and designed one of the covers. You could even start something yourself (such as a club). If the school has the resources and programs, it's a great idea.

Any last thoughts?

My best advice is to develop a strong style that is your own. If you love line art, make that your strength. Or if you love logos, make that the focus. You need to stand out.

Keep up to date with the digital programs that designers use: InDesign, Photoshop, Dreamweaver, etc. The Adobe Creative Cloud has a lot of options, for example. Be sure to keep on top of what's happening in that world: web designs, videos, and print.

Making High School Count

If you are still in high school or middle school, there are many things you can do now to help the postsecondary educational process go more smoothly. Consider these tips for your remaining years:

- Work on listening well and speaking and communicating clearly. Work on writing clearly and effectively.
- Learn how to learn. This means keeping an open mind, asking questions, asking for help when you need it, taking good notes, and doing your homework.
- Plan a daily homework schedule and keep up with it. Have a consistent, quiet place to study.
- Talk about your career interests with friends, family, and counselors. They may have connections to people in your community who you can shadow or who will mentor you.

- Try new interests and activities, especially during your first two years of high school.
- Be involved in extracurricular activities that truly interest you and say something about who you are and who you want to be.

Kids are under so much pressure these days to do it all, but you should think about working smarter rather than harder. If you are involved in things you enjoy, your educational load won't seem like such a burden. Be sure to take time for self-care, such as sleep, unscheduled down time, and activities that you find fun and energizing. See chapter 4 for more ways to relieve and avoid stress.

> "You have to be able to work under pressure. There are a lot of deadlines and the job can be stressful."—Kim Kultgen, graphic designer

Summary

This chapter looked at all the aspects of college and postsecondary schooling that you'll want to consider as you move forward. Remember that finding the right fit is especially important, as it increases the chances that you'll stay in school and finish your degree or program—and have an amazing experience while you're there.

In this chapter, you learned about how to find a good educational fit and how to get the best education for the best deal. You also learned a little about scholarships and financial aid, how the SAT and ACT work, and how to create a fantastic portfolio that eloquently expresses who you are and shows your talent.

Use this chapter as a jumping off point to dig deeper into your particular area of interest, but don't forget these important points:

- Take the SAT and ACT tests early in your junior year so you have time to take them again if you need to. Most schools automatically accept the highest scores.
- Make sure that the school you plan to attend has an accredited program in your field of study.

- Don't underestimate the importance of school visits, especially in pursuit of the right academic fit. Come prepared to ask questions not addressed on the school's website or in the literature.
- Your portfolio is a very important piece of your application that can set you apart from other applicants. Take the time and energy needed to make it unique and compelling.
- Don't assume you can't afford a school based on the sticker price. Many schools offer great scholarships and aid to qualified students. It doesn't hurt to apply. This advice especially applies to minorities, veterans, and students with disabilities.
- Don't lose sight of the fact that it's important to pursue a career that you enjoy, are good at, and are passionate about! You'll be a happier person if you do so.

At this point, your career goals and aspirations should be jelling. At the very least, you should have a plan for finding out more information. And don't forget about networking, which was covered in more detail in chapter 2. Remember to research the school or degree program before you reach out and especially before you visit. Faculty and staff find students who ask challenging questions much more impressive than those who ask questions that can be answered by spending ten minutes on the school website.

Chapter 4 goes into detail about the next steps—writing a résumé and cover letter, interviewing well, follow-up communications, and more. This information is not just for college grads; you can use it to secure internships, volunteer positions, summer jobs, and more. In fact, the sooner you can hone these communication skills, the better off you'll be in the professional world.

4

Writing Your Résumé and Interviewing

No matter what you aspire to be, having a well-written résumé and impeccable interviewing skills will help you reach your ultimate goals. This chapter provides some helpful tips and advice to build the best résumé, cover letter, and portfolio; how to interview well with all your prospective employers; and how to communicate effectively and professionally at all times. The advice in this chapter isn't just for people entering the workforce full-time, either; it can help you score an internship or summer job or help you give a great college interview to impress the admissions office.

After we talk about writing your résumé and building a great portfolio, the chapter discusses important interviewing skills that you can build and develop over time. The chapter also has some tips for dealing successfully with stress, which is an inevitable by-product of a busy life.

Writing Your Résumé

If you're a teen writing a résumé for your first job, you likely don't have a lot of work experience under your belt. Because of this limited work experience, you need to include classes and coursework that are related to the job you're seeking, any school activities and volunteer experience you have, and your best sample design work. While you are writing your résumé, you might discover some talents and recall some activities you did that you forgot about but that are still important to add. Think about volunteer work, side jobs you've held, organizations you've been a member of, and the like.

Visually, your résumé as a multimedia or graphic designer should be eye-catching and unique—more "out there" than the traditional résumé. With regard to content, the approach should be about the same as for other professions.[1]

71

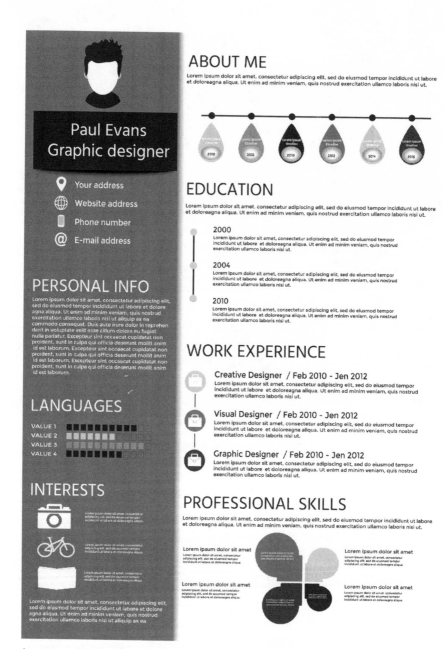

As someone in a visually creative field, your résumé should be visually unique and compelling.
©Tanyasun/iStock/Getty Images Plus

PARTS OF A RÉSUMÉ

The functional résumé is the best approach when you don't have a lot of pertinent work experience, as it is written to highlight your abilities rather than your experience. (The other, perhaps more common, type of résumé is called the chronological résumé, which lists a person's accomplishments in chronological order, most recent jobs listed first.) This section breaks down and discusses the functional résumé in greater detail.

Here are the essential parts of your résumé:

- *Heading:* This should include your name, address, and contact information, including phone, e-mail, and portfolio website if you have one.
- *Education:* Always list your most recent school or program first. Include date of completion (or expected date of graduation), degree or certificate earned, and the institution's name and address. Include workshops, seminars, and related classes here as well.
- *Skills:* Skills include computer literacy, leadership skills, organizational skills, and time-management skills. Be specific in this area, when possible.
- *Activities:* Activities can be related to skills. Perhaps an activity listed here helped you develop a skill listed above. This section can be combined with the Skills section, but it's often helpful to break these apart if you have enough substantive things to say in both areas. Examples include leadership roles, community service work, clubs and organizations, and so on.
- *Experience:* If you don't have any actual work experience that's relevant, you might consider skipping this section. However, you can list relevant design and website projects if you have relevant work to show.
- *Interests:* This section is optional, but it's a chance to include special talents and interests. Keep it short, factual, and specific.
- *Languages:* List all the scripting and programing languages you've used, as well as relevant software such as Photoshop, Acrobat, InDesign, and so on.
- *References:* It's best to say that references are available on request. If you do list actual contacts, list no more than three and make sure you inform them that they might be contacted.

The Skills, Interests, Experience, and Languages entries can be creatively combined or developed to maximize your abilities and experience. These are not set-in-stone sections that every résumé must have.

If you are applying for a job as designer (a web or multimedia designer in particular), it's a good idea to put together an online portfolio to show potential employers the work you've done in the past. Even if it was not professionally commissioned, it's an opportunity to show them your talent and range. See the section "Building Your Portfolio" later in this chapter for lots of good tips.

If you're still not seeing the big picture here, it's helpful to look at résumé and portfolio examples online to see how others have approached this process. Search for "graphic design résumé examples" or "example portfolios" to get a look at some examples.

RÉSUMÉ-WRITING TIPS

Regardless of your situation and why you're writing the résumé, here are some basic tips and techniques you should use:

- Keep it short, attractive, and compelling. Your design can be unique and clever, but make sure it doesn't get in the way of readability.
- Use simple language. Keep it to one page.
- Highlight your academic achievements, such as a high GPA (above 3.5) or academic awards. If you have taken classes related to the job you're interviewing for, list those briefly as well.
- Emphasize your extracurricular activities, internships, and the like. Use these activities to show your skills, interests, and abilities.
- Use action verbs, such as *led, designed, created, taught, ran,* and *developed.*
- Be specific and give examples.
- Always be honest.
- Include leadership roles and experience.
- Edit and proofread at least twice and have someone else do the same. Ask a professional (such as your school writing center or your local

library services) to proofread it for you also. Don't forget to run spell check.

- In some cases, include a cover letter (discussed next).

THE COVER LETTER

Every résumé you send out via standard mail should include a cover letter. This can be the most important part of your job search because it's often the first thing that potential employers read. By including the cover letter, you're showing potential employers that you took the time to learn about them and address them personally. This goes a long way to show that you're interested in the position.

Be sure to call the organization or verify on the website the name and title of the person to whom you should address the letter. This letter should be brief. Introduce yourself and begin with a statement that will grab the person's attention. Keep in mind that employers potentially receive hundreds of résumés and cover letters for every open position. You want yours to stand out. Important information to include in the cover letter, from the top, includes:

- The current date
- Your address and contact information
- The recipient's name, company name, and contact information
- Salutation

Then you begin the letter portion of the cover letter, which should mention how you heard about the position, something extra about you that will interest the potential employer, practical skills you can bring to the position, and past experience related to the job. You should apply the facts outlined in your résumé to the job to which you're applying. Each cover letter should be personalized for the position and company to which you're applying. Don't use "To whom it may concern"; instead, take the time to find out to whom you should actually address the letter. Finally, end with a complimentary closing, such as "Sincerely, Piper E. Smith" and be sure to add your signature. Search the internet for "sample cover letters for internships" or "sample cover letters for high schoolers" to see some good examples.

If you are e-mailing your résumé instead of printing it, you'll need to pay particular attention to the subject line of your e-mail. Be sure that it is specific to the position you are applying for. In fact, you should follow all the guidelines above for creating a cover letter when you write your introductory e-mail.

In all cases, it's really important to follow the employer's instructions on how to submit your cover letter and résumé. Generally speaking, it is better to send PDF documents rather than editable documents. For one, everyone can read a PDF, whereas they might not be able to read the version of Word that you used. Most word processing programs have an option under the Save command that allows you to save your work as a PDF.

LINKING IN WITH IMPACT

As well as your paper or electronic résumé, creating a LinkedIn profile is a good way to highlight your experience and promote yourself as well as to network. Joining professional organizations or connecting with other people in your desired field are good ways to keep abreast of changes and trends and work opportunities.

The key elements of a LinkedIn profile are your photo, your headline, and your profile summary. These are the most revealing parts of the profile and the ones employers and connections will base their impression of you on.

The photo should be carefully chosen. Remember that LinkedIn is not Facebook or Instagram: It is not the place to share a photo of you acting too casually on vacation or at a party. According to Joshua Waldman, author of *Job Searching with Social Media for Dummies*, the choice of photo should be taken seriously and be done right. His tips:

- Choose a photo in which you have a nice smile.
- Dress in professional clothing.
- Ensure the background of the photo is pleasing to the eye. According to Waldman, some colors—like green and blue—convey a feeling of trust and stability.
- Remember: it's not a mug shot. You can be creative with the angle of your photo rather than staring directly into the camera.
- Use your photo to convey some aspect of your personality.
- Focus on your face. Remember: visitors to your profile will see only a small thumbnail image, so be sure your face takes up most of it.[2]

Building Your Portfolio

As you learned in chapter 3, your portfolio is an important part of your application, as it allows you not only to showcase your work but to express who you are and how passionate you are about what you do. Your résumé is important, but your portfolio is where you really show your talent and your personal style. There are many online tools available—free and by subscription—that help you create a portfolio of your designs.

Your portfolio should be engaging and should demonstrate your strengths and passions as a designer.
©milindri/iStock/Getty Images Plus

Here are some of the main takeaways:

- Always keep your designs and portfolio site up to date.
- Most important: Always push yourself, and get critique and feedback from the most critical person you know.
- Don't distract from the work. Make your presentation about the ideas, images or designs, not the presentation's interface.
- The fewer clicks it takes before your gallery is presented, the better.
- Make sure your designs are relevant to the job you are applying for and don't be afraid to shuffle them to fit.

- Make it easy to find you. Your contact info should be easily accessible from any point on your materials.
- Never stop creating. Revamp your design every so often. Try to post something new as often as you can.
- Don't include anything but your *very best* work. Better ten designs that rock than a wide variety of samples that make your work quality look questionable.[3]

Come up with website concepts if you are interested in becoming a web developer. If you're an icon or logo designer, create some alternative logos for well-known brands. In other words, you don't need to have an official internship or job placement to gain experience you can use to impress potential employers (or college entrance boards with, if you're still in high school).

> "Go see graphic design in action in your town. Reach out to local designers or look on Craigslist to see who is advertising for designers in your area. Contact them and ask if you can come in and job shadow."—Danielle Foster

It's also a good idea to arrange to job shadow with a professional in the field, in whichever capacity you find most interesting to you. This means accompanying someone to work and observing the tasks they perform, the work culture, the environment, the hours, and the intensity of the work. Talk with people you know who work in the business.

Interviewing Skills

The best way to avoid nerves and keep calm when you're interviewing is to be prepared. It's okay to feel scared, but keep it in perspective. It's likely that you'll receive many more rejections than acceptances in your professional life, as we all do. However, you only need one *yes* to start out.

Think of the interviewing process as a learning experience. With the right attitude, you will learn from each one and get better with each subsequent interview. That should be your overarching goal. Consider these tips and tricks when interviewing, whether it be for a job, internship, college admission, or something else entirely[4]:

- Practice interviewing with a friend or relative. Practicing will help calm your nerves and make you feel more prepared. Ask for specific feedback from your friends. Do you need to speak more loudly? Are you making enough eye contact? Are you actively listening when the other person is speaking?
- Learn as much as you can about the company or organization, and be sure to understand the position for which you're applying. This will show the interviewer that you are motivated and interested in the organization.

    Speak up during the interview. Convey to the interviewer important points about yourself. Don't be afraid to ask questions. Try to remember the interviewers' names and call them by name. Consider these questions:

    o What created the need to fill this position? Is it a new position or has someone left the company?
    o Where does this position fit in the overall hierarchy of the organization?
    o What are the key skills required to succeed in this job?
    o What challenges might I expect to face within the first six months on the job?
    o How does this position relate to the achievement of the company's (or department's, or boss's) goals?
    o How would you describe the company culture?
- Arrive early and dress professionally and appropriately. (You can read more about proper dress in a following section.)
- Take some time to prepare answers to commonly asked questions. Be ready to describe your career or educational goals to the interviewer.

Common questions you may be asked during a job interview include:

- Tell me about yourself.
- What are your greatest strengths?
- What are your weaknesses?
- Tell me something about yourself that's not on your résumé.

- What are your career goals?
- How do you handle failure? Are you willing to fail?
- How do you handle stress and pressure?
- What are you passionate about?
- Why do you want to work for us?

Common questions you may be asked during a college admissions interview include these:

- Tell me about yourself.
- Why are you interested in going to college?
- Why do you want to major in this subject?
- What are your academic strengths?
- What are your academic weaknesses? How have you addressed them?
- What will you contribute to this college/school/university?
- Where do you see yourself in ten years?
- How do you handle failure? Are you willing to fail?
- How do you handle stress and pressure?
- Whom do you most admire?
- What is your favorite book?
- What do you do for fun?
- Why are you interested in this college/school/university?

Jot down notes about your answers to these questions, but don't try to memorize the answers. You don't want to come off as too rehearsed during the interview. Remember to be as specific and detailed as possible when answering these questions. Your goal is to set yourself apart in some way from the other interviewees. Always accentuate the positive, even when you're asked about something you did not like, or about failure or stress. Most importantly, though, be yourself.

Active listening is the process of fully concentrating on what is being said, understanding it, and providing nonverbal cues and responses to the person talking.[5]
It's the opposite of being distracted and thinking about something else when someone is talking. Active listening takes practice. You might find that your mind

wanders and you need to bring it back to the person talking (and this could happen multiple times during one conversation). Practice this technique in regular conversations with friends and relatives. In addition to helping you give a better interview, it can cut down on nerves and make you more popular with friends and family, as everyone wants to feel that they are really being heard. For more on active listening, check out www.mindtools.com/CommSkll/ActiveListening.htm.

You should also be ready to ask questions of your interviewer. In a practical sense, there should be some questions you have that you can't find the answer to on the website or in the literature. Also, asking questions shows that you are interested and have done your homework. Avoid asking questions about salary or special benefits at this stage, and don't ask about anything negative that you've heard about the company. Keep the questions positive and related to you and the position to which you're applying. Some example questions to potential employers include:

- What is a typical career path for a person in this position?
- How would you describe the ideal candidate for this position?
- How is the department organized?
- What kind of responsibilities come with this job? (Don't ask this if it has already been addressed in the job description or discussion.)
- What can I do as a follow-up?
- When do you expect to reach a decision?

See "Make the Most of Campus Visits" in chapter 3 for some good examples of questions to ask the college admissions office. The important thing is to write your own questions related to information you really want to know, and be sure your question isn't already answered on the website, in the job desctription, or in the literature. This will show genuine interest.

EFFECTIVELY HANDLING STRESS

As you're forging ahead with your life plans—whether it's college, a full-time job, or even a gap year—you might find that these decisions feel very important and heavy and that the stress is difficult to deal with. This is completely normal. Try these simple techniques to relieve stress:

- Take deep breaths in and out. Try this for thirty seconds. You'll be amazed at how it can help.
- Close your eyes and clear your mind.
- Go scream at the passing subway car. Or lock yourself in a closet and scream. Or scream into a pillow. For some people, this can really help.
- Keep the issue in perspective. Any decision you make now can be changed if it doesn't work out.

Want to know how to avoid stress altogether? It is surprisingly simple. Of course, simple doesn't always mean easy, but these ideas are basic and make sense based on what we know about the human body:

- Get enough sleep.
- Eat healthy.
- Get exercise.
- Go outside.
- Schedule downtime.
- Connect with friends and family.

The bottom line is that you need to take time for self-care. There will always be stress in life, but how you deal with it makes all the difference. This only becomes more important as you enter college or the workforce and maybe have a family. Developing good, consistent habits related to self-care now will serve you all your life.

Dressing Appropriately

It's important to determine what kind of dress is appropriate in the setting of the interview. What is appropriate in a large corporate setting might be different from what you'd expect at a small liberal arts college or at a creative design firm. For example, most college admissions offices suggest business casual attire, for example, but depending on the job interview, you may want to step it up from there. Again, it's important to do your homework and be prepared. In addition to reading up on the organization's guidelines, it never hurts to take a look around the website to see what other people are wearing to work or to interviews. Regardless of the setting, make sure your clothes are not wrinkled, untidy, or stained. Avoid revealing clothing of any kind.

Even something like "business casual" can be interpreted in many ways, so do some research to find out what exactly is expected of you. ©seb_ra/iStock/Getty Images Plus

Follow-Up Communication

Be sure to follow up, whether via e-mail or regular mail, with a thank-you note to the interviewer. This is true whether you're interviewing for a job or interviewing with a college. A handwritten thank-you note, posted in the mail, is best. In addition to showing consideration, it will trigger the interviewer's memory about you and it shows that you have genuine interest in the position, company, or school. Be sure to follow the business letter format and highlight the key points of your interview and experience at the company or school. Be prompt with your thank-you note! Put it in the mail the day after your interview or send it by e-mail the same day.

What Employers Expect

Regardless of the job, profession, or field, there are universal characteristics that all employers—and schools, for that matter—look for in candidates. At this early stage in your professional life, you have an opportunity to recognize which of these foundational characteristics are your strengths (and therefore highlight them in an interview) and which are weaknesses (and therefore continue to work on them and build them up). Consider these characteristics:

- Positive attitude
- Dependability
- Desire to continue to learn
- Initiative
- Effective communication
- Cooperation
- Organization
- Passion for the profession

This is not an exhaustive list, and other desirable characteristics can very well include things like creativity, sensitivity to others, honesty, good judgment, loyalty, responsibility, and punctuality. Consider these important characteristics when you answer the common questions that employers ask. It pays to work these traits into the answers—of course, being honest and realistic about yourself.

BEWARE WHAT YOU SHARE ON SOCIAL MEDIA

Most of us engage in social media. Sites such as Facebook, Twitter, and Instagram provide a platform for sharing photos and memories, opinions and life events, and reveal everything from our political stance to our sense of humor. It's a great way to connect with people around the world, but once you post something, it's accessible to anyone—including potential employers—unless you take mindful precautions.

Your posts may be public, which means you may be making the wrong impression without realizing it. More and more often, people are using search engines like Google to get a sense of potential employers, colleagues, or employees, and the impression you make online can have a strong impact on how you are perceived. According to the website Career Builder, 60 percent of employers search for information on candidates on social media sites.[6]

The website Glassdoor offers the following tips for how to keep your social media activity from sabotaging your career success:

1. Check your privacy settings. Ensure that your photos and posts are accessible only to the friends or contacts you want to see them. You want to come across as professional and reliable.
2. Rather than avoiding social media while searching for a job, use it to your advantage. Give future employees a sense of your professional interest by liking pages or joining groups of professional organizations related to your career goals.
3. Grammar counts. Be attentive to the quality of writing of all your posts and comments.
4. Be consistent. With each social media outlet, there is a different focus and tone of what you are communicating. LinkedIn is very professional while Facebook is far more social and relaxed. It's okay to take a different tone on various social media sites, but be sure you aren't blatantly contradicting yourself.
5. Choose your username carefully. Remember, social media may be the first impression anyone has of you in the professional realm.[7]

JILL FLORES: AN EXPERT IN MAGAZINE AND BOOK DESIGN

Jill Flores. *Courtesy of Jill Flores*

Jill Flores received her associate's degree in commercial art in 1988. Her first job was in publishing at Hitmakers magazine (a Top 40 magazine that is no longer in print). At that time, using computers to lay out print media was new. She was hired to help transition the magazine from the pasteup method to digital production. The magazine brought Macs in-house and trained her, and she helped it go digital. She was also the art director at National Dragster, a weekly magazine, for about seven and a half years. She helped that magazine go completely digital as well. She then started freelancing and worked mostly in book publishing for the next sixteen years. She also worked for a few different monthly magazines as a free-lancer.

Can you explain how you became interested in graphic design?

I always wanted to be an artist as a kid. I wanted to design greeting cards and wrapping paper. I created my own hand-drawn cards throughout high school. Initially, I wanted to be an illustrator. I graduated from college, landed into print publishing right away, and never got out of it!

Can you talk about your best job and why?

I really loved all the years I freelanced (took layout jobs on spec from various companies and laid them out at home on my own equipment). I could create my own schedule and got to be home with my child. And it was flexible. It was wonderful and I think I made the most money during that time as well (per hour), because I could be quick and the page rate was good, even though it wasn't always full-time. I could work whenever in the day it was best for me. However, it was inconsistent, and I couldn't count on work being there. There were no health benefits and no paid vacations. Also, I felt like I always had to say yes because I never knew when I would not have work. Sometimes I would work twenty or more hours in a day. But I didn't want to say no due to job insecurity. Having said all that, I still enjoyed my years freelancing the best.

Do you think education prepared you for your job?

Because of the era when I went to school, I didn't learn a single thing about graphic design on a computer! I learned all of that on the job. But what my schooling did give me was an in-depth understanding of design. We did everything by hand and it was all about composition and design principles. Today's students are so focused on the software and the computer aspects that the design is almost secondary to the tools. It's a different understanding of design.

When I was in school, I had a teacher who was a graphic designer. My college didn't have a graphic design degree then. Commercial art was the degree. He was a mentor to me and he advised me not to get a bachelor's degree (to stop at the associate's degree instead). He thought it was more important to get working and I could get better experience in two years working than I would get in college. I think that was valid advice at that time. But that didn't help me to get back in the industry after freelancing, and I find that now I can't apply for many posted jobs just because I don't have a bachelor's degree.

In today's world, you should finish your four-year degree and look into the certification programs. Being educated about all things web design is vitally important in being able to be employed.

What's the most surprising part of being a graphic artist?

When you are in school for graphic design, you get to be creative and you can take an assignment and create it like you envision it—colors, etc. In the real world, especially when freelancing, there isn't as much creativity. Even when you're creating a flyer or logo, you are still taking someone else's ideas and putting them together for them. You almost have to depersonalize it because you have to be ready for them not to like it. You can't be hurt by that or take it personally. This is not a reflection of you—it's for them and it's what they want. This was a huge lesson for me. The reality is that the job is not as creative as you'd like to think it is. You very often plug and chug elements into a predesigned template.

What are some things in this profession that are especially challenging right now?

Everything is web-based and the majority of the work is there now, not in print as much. My experience is mainly in print, but it's all web-based now.

What are some characteristics of a good graphic designer?

You need to be a good listener so you can understand your clients' needs and translate them appropriately. Your job as a graphic designer is to understand the client's message and translate that into a graphic design. You need to be able to know the target audience, understand the message, etc. A good work ethic is also important. And you must have a solid ego so you can take criticism.

What are some of the challenges of the job?

If you want to be a freelancer, you also have to be a good salesperson. You have to go out there and find new clients all the time. It takes energy and work and a different skill set.

What advice do you have for young people considering this career?

It's more important now than before to get your four-year (bachelor's) degree.

Also, be careful of your first job and make sure it's what you want to do. You might be stuck in that market and not be able to move because your experience is in only one area. My experience is that, in the graphic art world, you can easily get pigeonholed into an area and it's very hard to get work in a different area (such as moving from magazines to ad agencies).

Think about how long you stay somewhere. Stay maybe six months to get experience and then move to a different genre. It's not frowned upon as much in the early years to move jobs a lot in order to get a wide range of experience and work in different industries.

How can a young person prepare for a career in graphic design while in high school?

Actually consider how things are designed and think about what you like and don't like and why. Is it the colors, design, placement, and so on? Spend some time especially with web pages. Think about what works for you and what doesn't. Is it easy to navigate? In fact, think about this in everything you see. This builds the foundation of design. It's not just about how to make something—it's also how to make it look good.

Personal contacts can make the difference! Don't be afraid to contact designers and multimedia artists and other professionals you know. Personal connections can be a great way to find jobs and internship opportunities. Your high school teachers, your coaches and mentors, and your friends' parents are all examples of people who very well may know about jobs or opportunities that would suit you. Start asking several months before you hope to start a job or internship, because it will take some time to do research and arrange interviews. You can also use social media in your search. LinkedIn (www.linkedin.com), for example, includes lots of searchable information on local companies. Follow and interact with people on social media to get their attention. Just remember to act professionally and communicate with proper grammar, just as you would in person.

Summary

Well, you made it to the end of this book! Hopefully, you have learned enough about the multimedia and graphic design field to start along your journey or to continue along your path. If you've reached the end and you feel like design is your passion, that's great news. If you've figured out that it isn't the right field for you, that's good information to learn too. For many of us, figuring out what

With passion, creativity, and hard work, you can be a successful graphic designer! ©PeopleImages / E+/Getty Images

we *don't* want to do and what we *don't* like is an important step in finding the right career.

> "If anybody tells you you can't make a living at being an artist, don't listen. That's not true. You just have to try hard and not give up!"—Shawn Morningstar, graphic designer

There is a lot of good news about the multimedia and graphic design field. It's a great career choice for anyone with a passion for design. It's also a great career for people who get energy from working in creative settings. Job demand, especially for online design, is good. Having a plan and an idea about your future can help guide your decisions. After reading this book, you should be well on your way to having a plan for your future. Good luck to you as you move ahead!

Notes

Introduction

1. Bureau of Labor Statistics, United States Department of Labor, "Graphic Designers Outlook: Summary," https://www.bls.gov/ooh/arts-and-design/graphic-designers.htm.

2. Bureau of Labor Statistics, United States Department of Labor, "Multimedia Artists and Animators: Summary," https://www.bls.gov/ooh/arts-and-design/multimedia-artists-and-animators.htm.

3. Bureau of Labor Statistics, United States Department of Labor, "Web Developers: Summary," https://www.bls.gov/ooh/computer-and-information-technology/web-developers.htm.

4. Bureau of Labor Statistics, United States Department of Labor, "Graphic Designers: Job Outlook," https://www.bls.gov/ooh/arts-and-design/graphic-designers.htm#tab-6.

5. Ibid.

Chapter 1

1. Guru99, "What Is Backend Developer? Skills to Become a Web Developer," https://www.guru99.com/what-is-backend-developer.html.

2. The Art Institutes, "4 Different Types of Graphic Design Careers," https://www.artinstitutes.edu/about/blog/aig-4-different-types-of-graphic-design-careers.

3. Ibid.

4. Ibid.

5. Ibid.

6. Bureau of Labor Statistics, US Department of Labor, "Web Developers," https://www.bls.gov/ooh/computer-and-information-technology/web-developers.htm#tab-1.

7. Bureau of Labor Statistics, US Department of Labor, "Multimedia Artists and Animators," https://www.bls.gov/ooh/arts-and-design/multimedia-artists-and-animators.htm.

8. Bureau of Labor Statistics, US Department of Labor, "Graphic Designers," https://www.bls.gov/ooh/arts-and-design/graphic-designers.htm#tab-1.

9. Bureau of Labor Statistics, US Department of Labor, "Graphic Designers: Job Outlook," https://www.bls.gov/ooh/arts-and-design/graphic-designers.htm#tab-6.

10. Study.com, "How to Become a Video Game Designer," https://study.com/articles/How_to_Become_a_Video_Game_Designer_Education_and_Career_Roadmap.html.

11. Recruiter.com, "Career Outlook for Video Game Designers," https://www.recruiter.com/careers/video-game-designers/outlook/.

Chapter 2

1. Sheryl Burgstahler, Sara Lopez, and Scott Bellman, "Preparing for a Career: An Online Tutorial," DO-IT, https://www.washington.edu/doit/preparing-career-online-tutorial.

2. Daniella Alscher, "How to Build a Graphic Design Portfolio for the Clueless Beginner," G2 Learning Hub, March 28, 2019, https://learn.g2.com/graphic-design-portfolio.

3. Bureau of Labor Statistics, US Department of Labor, "Web Developers," https://www.bls.gov/ooh/computer-and-information-technology/web-developers.htm#tab-1.

4. Stephen Moyers, "Common Web Design Languages, What They Do and Why You Need Them," SpinX, https://www.spinxdigital.com/blog/common-web-design-languages-what-they-do-and-why-you-need-them/.

5. Bureau of Labor Statistics, US Department of Labor, "Graphic Designers," https://www.bls.gov/ooh/arts-and-design/graphic-designers.htm#tab-1.

6. Bureau of Labor Statistics, US Department of Labor, "How to Become a Graphic Designer," https://www.bls.gov/ooh/arts-and-design/graphic-designers.htm#tab-4.

7 Lou Adler, "New Survey Reveals 85% of All Jobs Are Filled via Networking," LinkedIn.com, February 29, 2016, https://www.linkedin.com/pulse/new-survey-reveals 85-all-jobs-filled-via-networking-lou-adler/.

8. Mathew Hilton, "Leverage Your Volunteering Experience When Applying to Physical Therapy School," CovalentCareers, May 11, 2016, https://covalentcareers.com/resources/volunteer-experience-physical-therapy-school/.

Chapter 3

1. Peter Van Buskirk, "Finding a Good College Fit," *U.S. News & World Report*, June 13, 2011, https://www.usnews.com/education/blogs/the-college-admissions-insider/2011/06/13/finding-a-good-college-fit.

2. National Center for Education Statistics, "Fast Facts: Graduation Rates," https://nces.ed.gov/fastfacts/display.asp?id=40.

3. US Department of Education, "Focusing Higher Education on Student Success," July 27, 2015, https://www.ed.gov/news/press-releases/fact-sheet-focusing-higher-education-student-success.

4. Gap Year Association, "Gap Year Data and Benefits," https://www.gapyearassociation.org/data-benefits.php.

5. Bureau of Labor Statistics, US Department of Labor, "How to Become a Graphic Designer," https://www.bls.gov/ooh/arts-and-design/graphic-designers.htm#tab-4.

6. CollegeBoard, "Understanding College Costs," https://bigfuture.collegeboard.org/pay-for-college/college-costs/understanding-college-costs.

7. Federal Student Aid, "Learn What's New with the FAFSA Process and Materials," Financial Aid Toolkit, https://financialaidtoolkit.ed.gov/tk/learn/fafsa/updates.jsp.

Chapter 4

1. Daniella Alscher, "Becoming a Graphic Designer: Skills, Job Titles + Career Tips," G2 Learning Hub, April 16, 2019, https://learn.g2.com/becoming-a-graphic-designer.

2. Joshua Waldman, *Job Searching with Social Media for Dummies* (Hoboken, NJ: Wiley, 2013), 149.

3. Karen DeFelice, "Create an Awesome Design Portfiolio with these 20 Pro Tips," Canva, https://www.canva.com/learn/portfolio/.

4. Justin Ross Muchnick, *Teens' Guide to College & Career Planning*, 12th ed. (Lawrenceville, NJ: Peterson's, 2015), 179–80.

5. Mind Tools, "Active Listening: Hear What People Are Really Saying," https://www.mindtools.com/CommSkll/ActiveListening.htm.

6. Career Builder, "Number of Employers Using Social Media to Screen Candidates Has Increased 500 Percent over the Last Decade," April 28, 2016, http://www.careerbuilder.com/share/aboutus/pressreleasesdetail.aspx?ed=12%2F31%2F2016&id=pr945&sd=4%2F28%2F2016.

7. Alice E. M. Underwood, "9 Things to Avoid on Social Media While Looking for a New Job," Glassdoor, January 3, 2018, https://www.glassdoor.com/blog/things-to-avoid-on-social-media-job-search/.

Glossary

2D animation: A type of animation in which the images are "flat," meaning they have width and height but no depth.

3D animation: A type of animation in which images appear in a 3D space, with width, height, and depth.

accreditation: The act of officially recognizing an organizational body, person, or educational facility as having a particular status or being qualified to perform a particular activity. For example, schools and colleges are accredited. *See also* **certification.**

ACT: One of the standardized college entrance tests that anyone wanting to enter undergraduate studies in the United States should take. It measures knowledge and skills in mathematics, English, reading, and science reasoning as they apply to college readiness. The ACT includes four multiple-choice sections and an optional writing test. The total score of the ACT is 36. *See also* **SAT.**

Adobe suite of products: The industry standard applications for many graphic design jobs, creations, and positions; includes Photoshop, Illustrator, Dreamweaver, Acrobat, and InDesign. *See each program separately for a full description of its purpose.*

Acrobat: An Adobe document-management program that enables users to create, edit, and manage documents in Portable Document Format (PDF). PDF documents look the same regardless of which operating system or hardware setup is used to view it.

animation: The art of creating electronic images with a computer in order to create moving images.

artist/animator: The person who creates environments and other animated, interactive images for designs.

associate's degree: A degree awarded by a community or junior college that typically requires two years of study.

bachelor's degree: An undergraduate degree awarded by a college or university that typically requires a four-year course of study when pursued full-time, but can vary by the degree earned and by the university awarding the degree.

body of work: All of the pieces ever made by a single artist (sometimes called the artist's *oeuvre*).

business model: A map for the successful creation and operation of a business, including sources of revenue, target customer base, products, and details of financing.

cascading stylesheets (CSS): A style sheet language used to format the layout of web pages. CSS control how a document written in a markup language like HTML appears in a browser and are considered more flexible, easier to use, and more versatile than HTML to format a web page.

certification: The action or process of confirming that an individual has acquired certain skills or knowledge, usually provided by some third-party review, assessment, or educational body. Individuals, not organizations, are certified. See also accreditation.

creative: Having the ability to make something that did not previously exist; also used in the business world to refer to a person who does creative work, such as a graphic artist or web designer.

critique: The process of describing and analyzing a work of art. In the classroom, critiques are a regular part of the learning process in which the teacher and other students give their responses to a particular piece and discuss its qualities, both positive and negative. It is a useful process for both those giving and receiving the critique.

criticism: The discussion or evaluation of a work of art, usually in terms of its perceived quality.

digital image: A computer file consisting of picture elements called pixels. High resolution digital images usually have at least 300 pixels per square inch at full size and are used for printed images. Low resolution digital images usually have 72 pixels per square inch and are used online. Common digital image types are JPG, PNG, TIFF, GIF, and PostScript.

doctoral degree: The highest level of degree awarded by colleges and universities. This degree qualifies the holder to teach at the university level and requires (usually published) research in the field. Earning a doctoral degree typically requires an additional three to five years of study after earning a bachelor's degree. Anyone with a doctorate degree—not just medical doctors—can be addressed as a "doctor."

Dreamweaver: An Adobe HTML editor that enables users to design and edit web pages. Like most of Adobe's products, it is geared toward use by professionals.

entrepreneur: A person who starts, organizes, and manages a business and is responsible for the financial risk involved.

freelancer: A person who works independently in a business providing services for a variety of clients.

gap year: A year between high school and college (or sometimes between college and postgraduate studies) during which the student is not in school but is instead involved in other pursuits, typically volunteer programs such as the Peace Corps, travel, or work and teaching.

general educational development (GED): A certificate earned by someone who has not gratuated from high school that is the equivalent to a high school diploma.

grants: Money to pay for postsecondary education that is typically awarded to students who have financial need, but can also be used in the areas of athletics, academics, demographics, veteran support, and special talents. Grants do not have to be paid back.

Hypertext Markup Language (HTML): A simple markup language used to control how web pages look in a browser. It can be enhanced by using cascading style sheets and scripting languages such as JavaScript.

Illustrator: An Adobe illustration and design tool that enables users to create and edit computer graphics images in the vector graphics format.

InDesign: An Adobe desktop publishing software that enables users to create and edit complex page layouts in a WYSIWYG ("what you see is what you get") environment. It runs on MacOS and Windows. *See also* QuarkXPress.

JavaScript: A common scripting language that runs in nearly all modern web browsers. It enables and runs complex features, such as displaying content updates, interactive maps, animated 2D/3D graphics and icons, scrolling boxes, and so on. Anything that is interactive or changes over time is likely controlled by JavaScript.

master's degree: A postgraduate degree awarded by colleges and universities that requires at least one additional year of study after obtaining a bachelor's degree. The degree holder shows mastery of a specific field.

multimedia art: Artwork created with new media technologies and computers.

online portfolio: An organized presentation of a designer's work in digital images on a website or social media site.

personal statement: A written description of your accomplishments, outlook, interests, goals, and personality that is an important part of your college application. The personal statement should set you apart from other applicants. The required length depends on the institution, but they generally range from one to two pages, or 500–1,000 words.

Photoshop: An Adobe illustration and design tool that enables users to create and edit computer graphics images in the raster graphics format (essentially, JPEG, PING, or GIF). Most of its features are built for editing and retouching digital photographs; however, Photoshop can also edit digital video frames, render text, create 3D modeling features, and develop design elements contents for websites. Like most of Adobe's products, it is geared toward use by professionals.

portfolio: A collection of pieces selected by the designer to share with potential clients or associates that best represents the designer's style and current work.

postsecondary degree: An educational degree above and beyond a high school education. This is a general description that includes trade certificates and certifications; associate's, bachelor's, and master's degrees; and beyond.

QuarkXPress: A Quark desktop publishing software that enables users to create and edit complex page layouts in a WYSIWYG ("what you see is what you get") environment. It runs on MacOS and Windows. *See also* InDesign.

SAT: One of the standardized tests in the United States that anyone applying to undergraduate studies should take. It measures verbal and mathematical reasoning abilities as they relate to predicting successful performance in college. It is intended to complement a student's GPA and school record in assessing readiness for college. The total score of the SAT is 1600. *See also* ACT.

scholarships: Merit-based aid used to pay for postsecondary education that does not have to be paid back. Scholarships are typically awarded based on academic excellence or some other special talent, such as music or art.

user experience (UX) design: A design process that focuses on creating a user experience that is favorable and even leads users to certain conclusions, such as a buying point. By creating user interactions that are pleasant and desirable, the design becomes meaningful and relevant to users. UX design usually considers aspects of branding, design, usability, and function.

user interface design: The visual layout of the actual elements (such as buttons, icons, lists, and graphics) that users can interact with on a website or technological product. This often refers to the visual layout of a web page or smartphone screen.

wireframe layout: A visual guide that shows the skeletal framework of a design piece such as a website. Wireframes are created to help visualize and arrange elements before the details are added. For websites, wireframes usually show which elements will exist on which pages. This is different from a mock-up, which usually shows more visual details (such as colors, type used, and other elements).

Resources

*A*re you looking for more information about the graphic design profession or about a particular area of study within the profession? Do you want to know more about the college application process or need some help finding the right educational fit for you? Do you want a quick way to search for a good college or school? Try these resources as a starting point on your journey toward finding a fulfilling career in graphic and multimedia design!

Books

Bayles, David, and Ted Orland. *Art & Fear: Observations on the Perils (and Rewards) of Artmaking.* Santa Barbara, CA: Capra Press, 1993.

Bolles, Richard N. *What Color Is Your Parachute? 2019: A Practical Manual for Job Hunters and Career Changers,* rev. ed. New York: Ten Speed Press, 2018.

Cameron, Julia. *The Artist's Way: A Spiritual Path to Higher Creativity.* New York: Jeremy P. Tarcher/Putnam, 2002.

Davis, Meredith. *Graphic Design Theory.* London: Thames & Hudson, 2012.

Fiske, Edward. *Fiske Guide to Colleges.* Naperville, IL: Sourcebooks, 2018.

King, Stephen. *On Writing: A Memoir of the Craft.* New York: Pocket Books/ Simon & Schuster, 2000.

Muchnick, Justin Ross. *Teens' Guide to College & Career Planning,* 12th ed. Lawrenceville, NJ: Peterson's, 2015.

Princeton Review. The Best 382 Colleges, 2018 Edition: Everything You Need to Make the Right College Choice. New York: Princeton Review, 2018.

Scher, Paula. *Works.* London: Unit Editions Studio, 2017.

Websites

Association for Computing Machinery's Special Interest Group on Computer Graphics (ACM SIGGRAPH) www.siggraph.org

Based in New York, the Association for Computing Machinery's Special Interest Group on Computer Graphics was founded in 1969. Its SIGGRAPH conference, held every year, is attended by tens of thousands of computer professionals. It has nearly one hundred thousand members from 190 different countries. Membership includes access to job postings, to other members, and to its many magazines, special interest groups, and periodicals.

American Gap Year Association

www.gapyearassociation.org

The American Gap Year Association's mission is "making transformative gap years an accessible option for all high school graduates." A gap year is a year taken between high school and college to travel, teach, work, volunteer, generally mature, and otherwise experience the world. The website has lots of advice and resources for anyone considering taking a gap year.

American Institute of Graphic Arts

www.aiga.org

Calling itself *the* professional association for design and boasting more than twenty-five thousand members in the United States, the American Institute of Graphic Arts is the oldest and largest professional organization for designers. Membership in the AIGA includes access to job postings, discounts on Creative Group services, health insurance assistance, access to its directory of designers, ability to post your portfolio at the site, and timely connection to the design community in terms of news and updates.

The Balance

www.thebalance.com

This site is all about managing money and finances, but also has a large section called Your Career, which provides advice for writing résumés and cover letters, interviewing, and more. Search the site for teens and you can find teen-specific advice and tips.

The College Entrance Examination Board

www.collegeboard.org

The College Entrance Examination Board tracks and summarizes financial data from colleges and universities all over the United States. This great, well-organized site can be your one-stop shop for all things college research. It contains lots of advice and information about taking and doing well on the SAT and ACT, many articles on college planning, a robust college search feature, a scholarship search feature, and a major and career search area. You can type your career of interest (for example, graphic design) into the search box and get back a full page that describes the career; gives advice on how to prepare, where to get experience, and how to pay for it; describes the characteristics you should have to excel in this career; lists of helpful classes to take while in high school; and lots of links for more information.

College Grad Career Profiles
www.collegegrad.com/careers
Although this site is primarily geared toward college graduates, the careers profiles area, indicated above, has a list of links to nearly every career you could ever think of. A single click takes you to a very detailed, helpful section that describes the job in detail, explains the educational requirements, includes links to good colleges that offer this career and to actual open jobs and internships, describes the licensing requirements (if any), lists salaries, and much more.

Education Planner
www.educationplanner.org
This site—which includes sections for students, parents, and counselors—breaks down the task of planning your career goals into simple, easy-to-understand steps. You can find personality assessments, get tips for preparing for school, read Q&As from counselors, download and use a planner worksheet, read about how to finance your education, and more.

GoCollege
www.gocollege.com
Calling itself the number one college-bound website on the internet, GoCollege provides lots of good tips and information about getting money and scholarships for college and getting the most out of your college education. This site also includes a good section on how scholarships in general work.

Go Overseas

www.gooverseas.com

Go Overseas claims to be your guide to more than fourteen thousand study and teach abroad programs that will change how you see the world. The site also includes information about high school abroad programs and gap year opportunities, and includes community reviews and information about finding programs specific to your interests and grade-level teaching aspirations, for example, information about the best countries for teaching English abroad.

Khan Academy

www.khanacademy.org

The Khan Academy website is an impressive collection of articles, courses, and videos about many educational topics in math, science, and the humanities. You can search any topic or subject (by subject matter and grade), and read lessons, take courses, and watch videos to learn all about it. The site includes test prep information for the SAT, ACT, AP, GMAT, and other standardized tests. There is also a College Admissions tab with lots of good articles and information, provided in the approachable Khan style.

Live Career Website

www.livecareer.com

This site has an impressive number of resources directed toward teens for writing résumés and cover letters, as well as interviewing.

Mapping Your Future

www.mappingyourfuture.org

This site helps young people figure out what they want to do and maps out how to reach career goals. Includes helpful tips on résumé writing, job hunting, job interviewing, and more.

Monster.com

www.monster.com

Monster.com is perhaps the most well-known and certainly one of the largest employment websites in the United States. You fill in a couple of search boxes and away you go. You can sort by job title, of course, as well as by company name, location, salary range, experience range, and much more. The site also includes information about career fairs, advice on résumés and interviewing, and more.

Occupational Outlook Handbook
www.bls.gov
The US Bureau of Labor Statistics produces this website, which offers lots of relevant and updated information about various careers, including average salaries, how to work in the industry, job market outlook, typical work environments, and what workers do on the job. See www.bls.gov/emp/ for a full list of employment projections.

Peace Corps
www.peacecorps.gov
If you are interested in taking a gap year before taking the next step in your career or education, consider joining the Peace Corps. Volunteers have the experience of working on projects that relate to health, agriculture, education, and youth and development, just to name a few, and the experience can help you find your passion and understand what the next step in your life should be.

Peterson's College Prep
www.petersons.com
In addition to lots of information about preparing for the ACT and SAT and easily searchable information about scholarships nationwide, the Peterson's site includes a comprehensive search feature for universities and schools based on location, major, name, and more.

Princeton Review Website
www.princetonreview.com/quiz/career-quiz
This site includes a very good aptitude test geared toward high schoolers to help them determine their interests and find professions that complement those interests.

Study.com
www.study.com
Similar to Khan Academy, Study.com allows you to search any topic or subject and read lessons, take courses, and watch videos to learn all about it.

TeenLife
www.teenlife.com
This site calls itself "the leading source for college preparation" and includes lots of information about summer programs, gap year programs, community service, and more. Promoting the belief that spending time out "in the world" outside of the classroom can help students develop important life skills, this site contains lots of links to volunteer and summer programs.

U.S. News & World Report *College Rankings*
www.usnews.com/best-colleges
U.S. News & World Report provides almost fifty different types of numerical rankings and lists of colleges throughout the United States to help students with their college search. You can search colleges by best reviewed, best value for the money, best liberal arts schools, best schools for B students, and more.

About the Author

Kezia Endsley is an editor and author from Indianapolis, Indiana. In addition to editing technical publications and writing books for teens, she enjoys running and triathlons, traveling, reading, and spending time with her family and many pets.

EDITORIAL BOARD